KeyShot 3D Rendering

Showcase your 3D models and create hyperrealistic images with KeyShot in the fastest and most efficient way possible

Jei Lee Jo

[PACKT]
PUBLISHING

BIRMINGHAM - MUMBAI

KeyShot 3D Rendering

Copyright © 2012 Packt Publishing

All rights reserved. No part of this book may be reproduced, stored in a retrieval system, or transmitted in any form or by any means, without the prior written permission of the publisher, except in the case of brief quotations embedded in critical articles or reviews.

Every effort has been made in the preparation of this book to ensure the accuracy of the information presented. However, the information contained in this book is sold without warranty, either express or implied. Neither the author, nor Packt Publishing, and its dealers and distributors will be held liable for any damages caused or alleged to be caused directly or indirectly by this book.

Packt Publishing has endeavored to provide trademark information about all of the companies and products mentioned in this book by the appropriate use of capitals. However, Packt Publishing cannot guarantee the accuracy of this information.

First published: December 2012

Production Reference: 1181212

Published by Packt Publishing Ltd.
Livery Place
35 Livery Street
Birmingham B3 2PB, UK.

ISBN 978-1-84969-482-7

www.packtpub.com

Cover Image by Abhishek Pandey (abhishek.pandey1210@gmail.com)

Credits

Author
  Jei Lee Jo

Reviewers
  Josh Mings
  Marlon Muñoz

Acquisition Editor
  Wilson D'souza

Commissioning Editor
  Yogesh Dalvi

Technical Editors
  Devdutt Kulkarni
  Kirti Pujari

Copy Editors
  Aditya Nair
  Alfida Paiva

Project Coordinator
  Esha Thakker

Proofreader
  Martin Diver

Indexer
  Monica Ajmera Mehta

Production Coordinator
  Melwyn D'sa

Cover Work
  Melwyn D'sa

About the Author

Jei Lee Jo, as a young child, had a passion for science fiction, fantasy worlds, and games. He lived mostly in Venezuela "before he moved to the United States in 2003. While in Venezuela, he studied biology sciences at La Universidad de los Andes During this period, he also worked as a Lab Technician, designing media tools and maquettes. After arriving in the United States, Jei became a Designer and CG Modeler at San Jose State University, where his aim was to always find a path where science and art co-exist in balance, and where each field supports the other in creating tools that are not only attractive and beautiful, but also practical. He currently works as Clinical Specialist 3D Modeler at Stryker OtisMed and has clients from industries such as Electronic Arts and Cisco Systems.

> This book is especially dedicated to Siu Lee, for her undying support, love, and care to help in the completion of this project. Also to Nam Lee, for always keeping a positive attitude and smiling even through the toughest times. To Dan Lee, for all his advice, knowledge, and for being the best brother one could ask for. Lastly, special thanks to Tian Jiao for never giving up and always being there when we all needed her the most.

About the Reviewers

Josh Mings is the Marketing Manager for Luxion, Inc., creators of KeyShot. He holds a Bachelor's degree in Mechanical Engineering Technology and Design from LeTourneau University. He is a CSWP and a certified SolidWorks Instructor. He is a Co-founder of EvD Media, Editor of `SolidSmack.com`, and a Co-host of `EngineerVsDesigner.com`, a weekly podcast about design, engineering, and what makes it all happen. As a father of four children, teaching and instructing others is his passion, as is discovering new methods to create and explore ways in which technology advances product development.

Marlon Muñoz is a Manager Interactive Developer and Lead 3D and Motion Designer at SapientNitro, where he helped in building and initiating the CG Department. He is also the FX Director and Founder of MM2 Media, Inc., where he continues to push boundaries in creating high-end 3D and FX for clients around the world. His designer background was the catalyst for him to continue developing his knowledge in the creative world while attending Miami International University of Art and Design, graduating with honors while majoring in Visual Effects and Motion Graphics. His organization, structure, and keen eye for detail are essential, as he specializes in 3D lighting, shading, rendering, and FX.

His work has been featured on various sites, including `motionserved.com` and `inspirations.cgrecord.net`, among others.

Marlon currently lives in Miami, FL with his beautiful wife Melissa.

www.PacktPub.com

Support files, eBooks, discount offers and more

You might want to visit `www.PacktPub.com` for support files and downloads related to your book.

Did you know that Packt offers eBook versions of every book published, with PDF and ePub files available? You can upgrade to the eBook version at `www.PacktPub.com` and as a print book customer, you are entitled to a discount on the eBook copy. Get in touch with us at `service@packtpub.com` for more details.

At `www.PacktPub.com`, you can also read a collection of free technical articles, sign up for a range of free newsletters and receive exclusive discounts and offers on Packt books and eBooks.

PACKTLIB®

`http://PacktLib.PacktPub.com`

Do you need instant solutions to your IT questions? PacktLib is Packt's online digital book library. Here, you can access, read and search across Packt's entire library of books.

Why Subscribe?

- Fully searchable across every book published by Packt
- Copy and paste, print and bookmark content
- On demand and accessible via web browser

Free Access for Packt account holders

If you have an account with Packt at `www.PacktPub.com`, you can use this to access PacktLib today and view nine entirely free books. Simply use your login credentials for immediate access.

Table of Contents

Preface — 1
Chapter 1: KeyShot's Overview — 5
  Introducing KeyShot — 5
  KeyShot versus traditional rendering programs — 6
  Getting started — 7
  Importing projects — 8
  The interface — 10
    Scene — 10
    Material — 11
      Material properties window — 12
    Environment — 13
      Environment properties window — 14
  Summary — 15
Chapter 2: Understanding Materials and Textures — 17
  Placing and editing materials — 18
    Pad — 18
    Tablet case — 19
    Buttons — 20
      Transparent cover — 22
      Adding a label — 25
      USB cable — 26
      Wacom stylus — 28
  Understanding materials and their properties — 32
    Texture properties — 35
    Labels tab — 40
  How to create materials — 42
    Plastics — 42
      Creating glass using plastic — 43
    Metals — 44

Table of Contents

Glass	44
Advanced	44
Texturing materials and methods	**45**
Summary	**50**
Chapter 3: Lighting Made Easy	**51**
Setting up our scene	**51**
Lighting properties	**56**
HDRI editor	60
Real-time settings	62
Working with cameras	**65**
Camera attributes	70
Insulated cup	**74**
Duplicating models	**80**
Summary	**83**
Chapter 4: Showcasing and Product Presentation	**85**
Preparing our project	**85**
Rendering in KeyShot	**89**
Output menu	90
Quality menu	90
Queue menu	91
Region menu	92
Network menu	92
Creating a turntable presentation	**93**
Summary	**96**
Chapter 5: Adding Effects with Photoshop	**97**
Replacing our background	**97**
Summary	**102**
Appendix: Command Lists and Hotkeys	**103**
Shortcuts menu	**103**
Files and documents	103
Toggling	103
Space and environment	104
Camera hotkeys	104
General hotkeys	104
Material hotkeys	105
Animation hotkeys	105
Real-time hotkeys	105
Index	**107**

Preface

KeyShot 3D Rendering is a quick startup guide designed for any beginners or professionals that want to create hyperrealistic images off their 3D models. The book contains various exercises that are specific to each chapter, which helps to clarify any concepts, definitions, or methods of usage that have been mentioned in the chapters. It will also cover and explain each of the parameters found inside KeyShot and how materials, lighting, and staging work together to deliver the most efficient and accurate results off our models.

This book addresses all the necessary steps to create fully rendered images, specifically from importing models to KeyShot until the final stage of outputting rendered images. It is not meant to examine or to teach 3D modeling techniques nor to create complex animations and special effects.

What this book covers

Chapter 1, KeyShot's Overview, explains the advantages and disadvantages that KeyShot offers, as a rendering application. It also covers all the steps for importing our models into the scene and familiarizing ourselves with the navigation menus.

Chapter 2, Understanding Materials and Textures, discusses the material and texture application procedures used for various exercises, as well as definitions of the parameters found in the material menu.

Chapter 3, Lighting Made Easy, covers the different properties found within the lighting menu in KeyShot. It also shows how to create our own lighting setup, and explains how materials and textures are directly influenced by our lighting. The camera setting is also discussed in this chapter.

Preface

Chapter 4, Showcasing and Product Presentation, demonstrates various methods and suggestions on how to present our work by changing certain lighting properties or creating different staging scenarios. It also discusses the settings found in the Rendering tab, as well as tips on how to improve lighting and reflections in our models.

Chapter 5, Adding Effects with Photoshop, shows an alternative way of illustrating how to stage and add effects to our rendered images from KeyShot.

Appendix, Command Lists and Hotkeys, includes a list of all the shortcuts and hotkeys for KeyShot.

What you need for this book

You will need the following for this book:

- A full or trial version of KeyShot 3 for Windows or Mac
- Lesson files for each chapter
- Adobe Photoshop CS3 or newer

Who this book is for

This book is intended for readers with intermediate or advanced knowledge of 3D modeling and texturing. There will be omissions made to certain exercises, and repetitive instructions or statements to minimize redundancy. It is also assumed that the readers have some previous experience in working with 3D applications such as Maya, 3ds Max, or SolidWorks.

Conventions

In this book, you will find a number of styles of text that distinguish between different kinds of information. Here are some examples of these styles, and an explanation of their meaning.

Code words in text are shown as follows: "We can choose a file such as `mesh_circular_normal.jpg` or similar."

New terms and **important words** are shown in bold. Words that you see on the screen, in menus or dialog boxes for example, appear in the text like this: "Find the material, **Plastic Hard white rough** by selecting **Plastic | Hard | Rough | Basic | Hard white rough**."

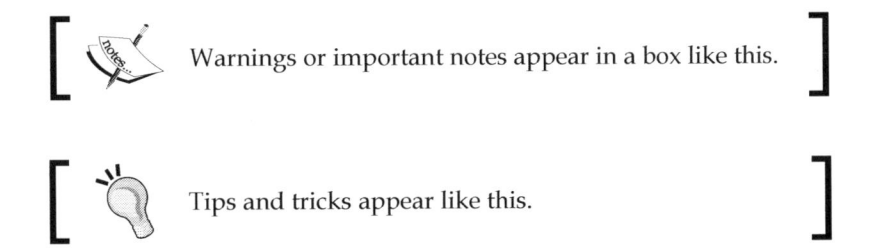

> Warnings or important notes appear in a box like this.

> Tips and tricks appear like this.

Reader feedback

Feedback from our readers is always welcome. Let us know what you think about this book—what you liked or may have disliked. Reader feedback is important for us to develop titles that you really get the most out of.

To send us general feedback, simply send an e-mail to feedback@packtpub.com, and mention the book title via the subject of your message.

If there is a topic that you have expertise in and you are interested in either writing or contributing to a book, see our author guide on www.packtpub.com/authors.

Customer support

Now that you are the proud owner of a Packt book, we have a number of things to help you to get the most from your purchase.

Downloading the example code

You can download the example code files for all Packt books you have purchased from your account at http://www.PacktPub.com. If you purchased this book elsewhere, you can visit http://www.PacktPub.com/support and register to have the files e-mailed directly to you.

Errata

Although we have taken every care to ensure the accuracy of our content, mistakes do happen. If you find a mistake in one of our books—maybe a mistake in the text or the code—we would be grateful if you would report this to us. By doing so, you can save other readers from frustration and help us improve subsequent versions of this book. If you find any errata, please report them by visiting http://www.packtpub.com/support, selecting your book, clicking on the **errata submission form** link, and entering the details of your errata.

Once your errata are verified, your submission will be accepted and the errata will be uploaded on our website, or added to any list of existing errata, under the Errata section of that title. Any existing errata can be viewed by selecting your title from http://www.packtpub.com/support.

Piracy

Piracy of copyright material on the Internet is an ongoing problem across all media. At Packt, we take the protection of our copyright and licenses very seriously. If you come across any illegal copies of our works, in any form, on the Internet, please provide us with the location address or website name immediately so that we can pursue a remedy.

Please contact us at copyright@packtpub.com with a link to the suspected pirated material.

We appreciate your help in protecting our authors, and our ability to bring you valuable content.

Questions

You can contact us at questions@packtpub.com if you are having a problem with any aspect of the book, and we will do our best to address it.

KeyShot's Overview

Rendering in KeyShot is one of the easiest and most intuitive ways of creating professional presentations of our projects. In this chapter we will learn how to import our projects into KeyShot and consider the advantages and limitations it has over traditional rendering packages.

In this chapter you will learn the following:

- KeyShot's basics and fundamentals
- Importing projects
- Getting familiar with the interface

Introducing KeyShot

Formerly known as HyperShot, KeyShot is an application developed by the company Luxion, that is run today by professionals in various disciplines to deliver images with hyperrealistic quality. KeyShot delivers physically accurate lighting and a library of materials that allow us to experiment and make changes all through our viewport in real time.

Whether we are engineers, artists, or designers, time is a precious element that we are always racing against, and this is particularly true when it comes to rendering 3D data. On some occasions, the quality of our work is compromised as we need to spend time learning complex new software. KeyShot has been designed with simplicity in mind, allowing the user to create high-quality images while putting aside the technical details.

Unlike other rendering packages on the market, KeyShot is a processor-based rendering program. All the rendering calculations are 100 percent CPU-based, which means we don't need a high-performance graphics card to get the job done. KeyShot utilizes all the cores and threads in your processor, and because it was built on 64-bit architecture, it also gives us more room to increase performance.

KeyShot versus traditional rendering programs

In order to work properly, it is important to have the right tools. KeyShot allows you to apply materials, set up the lighting, and obtain hyperrealistic images in a matter of minutes. Traditional rendering applications often have, too many settings, each giving the user a different level of control over the appearance of the project. Although a large number of settings allows for more flexibility, understanding how each of them works can be a time-consuming process.

In this section, we have laid out several points that we consider helpful when using KeyShot for your projects compared to other rendering applications.

The following are some basic points related to working with KeyShot:

- Workflow—import your 3D data, apply and fine-tune your textures and materials, set up your lighting, find your preferred camera view, and then render.
- KeyShot is fully integrated, just like any other rendering application, but it's been designed to be user friendly. You will find that most menu tabs and preferences are intuitive and easy to understand. It offers different arrays of mapping options, such as cylindrical, box shaped, spherical, or using UV coordinates, depending on your preference.
- It uses the **high dynamic range imaging (HDRI)** method to produce realistic lighting conditions.
- It provides physically accurate materials based on real-world properties. Each material found in KeyShot's library has been set up to produce a specific type of look when applied. This allows you to save time fine-tuning your materials for that specific look.
- It offers basic animation tools that allow you to set up professional presentations.

The following are a few basic points related to traditional rendering tools:

- They require some experience in rendering techniques, and they often have a steep learning curve.
- The user interfaces are cluttered with options and preferences and can be intimidating for first-time users.
- They are more flexible in terms of controlling the look of each individual feature of your project. The settings are broken down and laid out separately, allowing you to control everything from the number of lights and shadows per scene to the look of a material. A consequence of this, however, is that, there are more opportunities for errors and users are often overwhelmed by the amount of settings and controls.
- Materials and lighting are not always physically accurate. Reproducing a particular type of material or lighting setup is often time-consuming.
- They provide more robust animation tools and often include a rigging system, which allows for more complex animations.

KeyShot is a powerful rendering tool that is used in a variety of fields within the CG industry. However, it is important to remember that KeyShot has a limited set of animation tools, and I recommend using a different application such as Maya, 3ds Max, or Softimage if your project requires complex character animations or special effects.

Getting started

Now that we understand the fundamentals of KeyShot and its benefits, we will take a look at how to start using KeyShot for your projects, from the beginning to the end. If you do not have KeyShot, you can download a trial version from the website by performing the following steps:

1. Go to `http://www.keyshot.com/try/`.
2. Select your operating system (**Windows 32-bit**, **Windows 64-bit**, or **Mac OS X**) and download it.
3. Install your trial version and select **Continue without registering**.

KeyShot's Overview

Importing projects

KeyShot supports a variety of file formats from third-party applications. A list of the files currently supported can be found on the KeyShots website. For our projects, we will be working with files with the OBJ (object file) extension. Let's go ahead and get started. Perform the following steps:

1. Open KeyShot.
2. At the bottom of your viewport, you will see six icons—**Import**, **Library**, **Project**, **Animation**, **Screenshot**, and **Render**, as shown in the following screenshot:

3. Go ahead and click on **Import**.
4. Let's choose our lesson file, `Wacom_2`, from the `data` folder.
5. A new window for configuring imported files will appear.

The new settings window allows you to choose the orientation or the direction in which your 3D object will be placed in the viewport. Depending on which application we are importing our files to, some of them have their Cartesian axis orientation set up differently. In this case, the file we will be working with is an OBJ file imported from Maya, and this file has **Y Up** as its **Orientation**, as shown in the following screenshot:

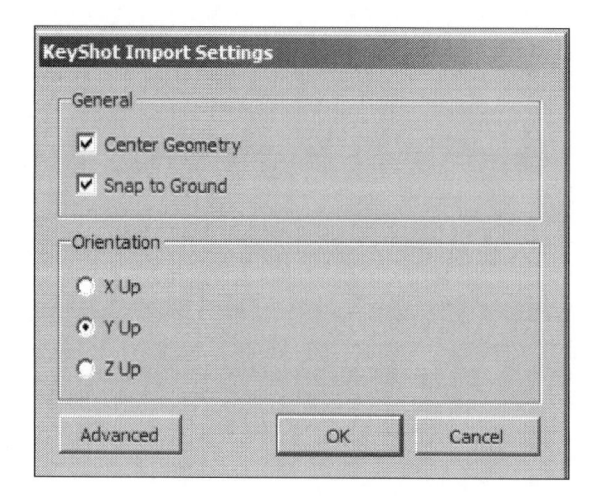

When working with our project files in KeyShot, it is important to remember prior to importing any models that, all parts of the model need to have their own material assigned to them. To do this, before exporting any of our 3D files from other applications, make sure that the option material is checked in the export options. Once all the pieces of our model have been assigned with their own material, KeyShot will be able to understand how to assign materials properly to all parts of the mesh. A new feature called **Material Template**, currently available in KeyShot v3.3 and later versions, allows us to link materials and parts of our models to the materials found inside KeyShot's library. For example, instead of copying and pasting materials from one object to another, we can create a template that automatically applies all the materials to the corresponding parts of a model when it is imported into the scene.

When creating a template, we need to specify a source name and a destination name. The source name is essentially the name of the part or the material exported directly from a third-party application such as Maya or SolidWorks. Once it is added to the template list, KeyShot will search for any parts or materials associated with the names in the source list and apply any assigned materials in the destination list. We can see an example of a template list in the following screenshot, with the parts of our Wacom tablet listed on the left-hand side and the materials we assigned them with on the right-hand side:

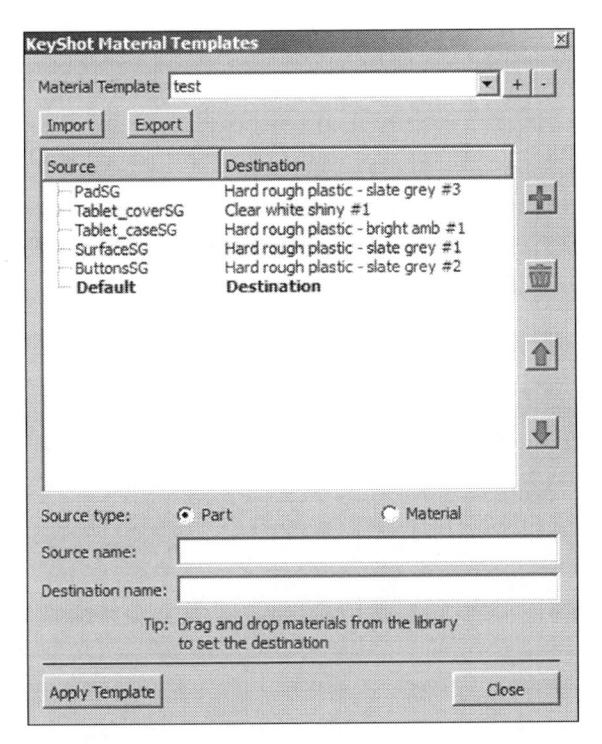

Next, let's see how to move, rotate, or scale our model in the viewport. Perform the following steps to do so:

1. Right-click on the model.
2. A new selection box will appear; choose to either move a part of the object or the entire object.
3. When working with a mesh that has multiple parts, it is good practice to hide the parts we don't currently need. To do this, simply right-click on the part we wish to hide and select the **Hide Part** option from the new menu.

The interface

Once our project model has been imported, our 3D file should be displayed in our viewport along with a new project window. This window contains five different tabs, of which we will discuss three in the following sections.

Scene

The **Scene** tab shows all the parts of our model. The left-hand side of our **Project** window shows the parts of our mesh under the **Parts** heading. The order and the name of each of the parts are listed according to the name of the material that was assigned to it by its original application. In this case, our 3D tablet was imported from Maya and all its parts were assigned with a specific material inside Maya. The right-hand side of our **Project** window shows the list of the current materials that have been applied to the parts inside KeyShot under the **Materials** heading, as shown in the following screenshot:

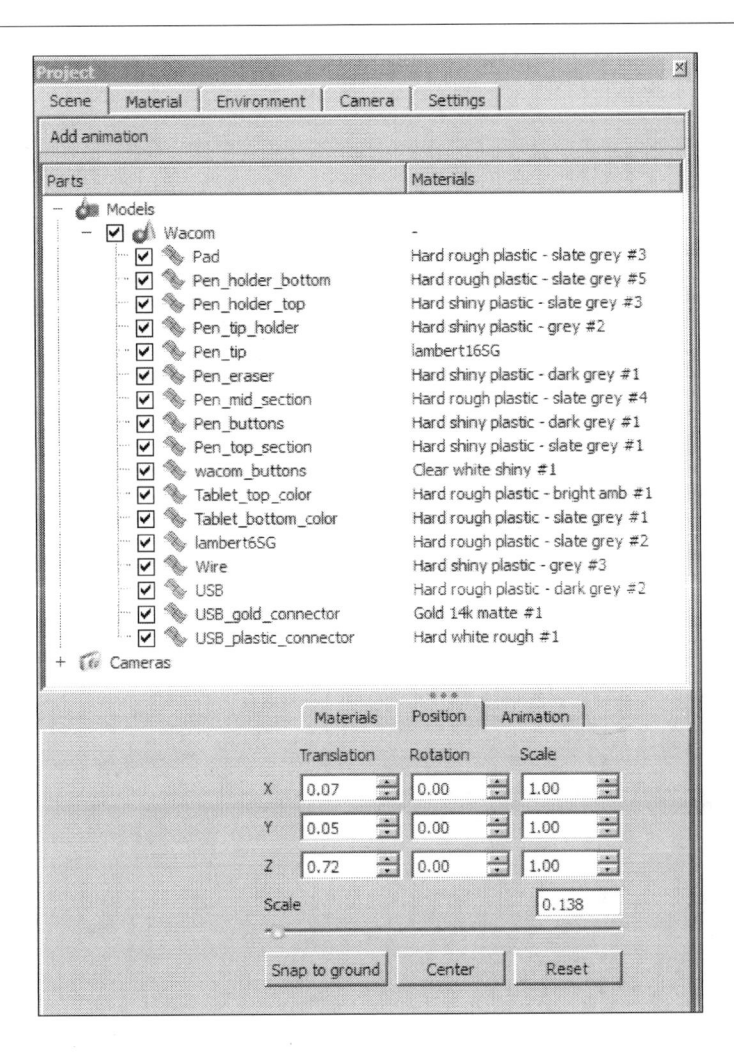

Material

The **Material** tab lists all the available materials in KeyShot according to their category. In the lower part of our **Project** window, we can see the materials that belong to the specific folder we have chosen from the list. To apply any material to our model, simply drag the material and drop it onto the part of our model where we wish to apply it. Another way of accessing the list of materials is by clicking on the **Library** tab in our main viewport.

KeyShot's Overview

If we need to access the material properties of a specific part of our model, we can do so by double-clicking on any part of the model.

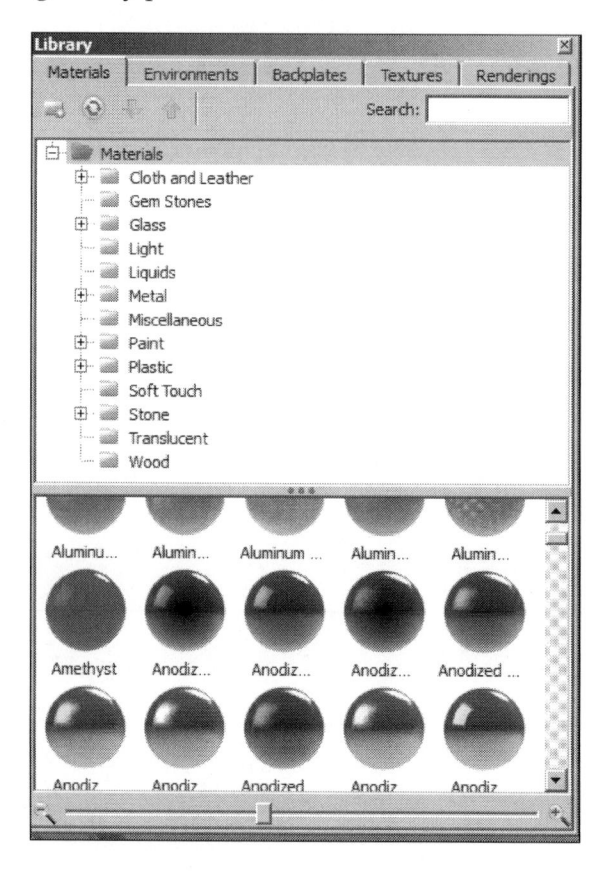

To apply any material to our project, we perform the following steps:

1. Open the **Library** window by clicking on the **Library** icon from the viewport menu.
2. Drag the desired material and drop it onto our project.
3. Double-click on our model with the applied material to open the **Material Properties** window.

Material properties window

The material properties window allows us to modify the attributes of the material we choose. Depending on the material, certain properties will be available for us to modify. For example, any glass models will have the refraction attribute, which won't be available to us if we choose a metallic shader. In general, we have to fine-tune the properties of the materials in order to reproduce the look of real-life materials for most 3D applications such as Maya or 3ds Max. In KeyShot, however, this is no longer necessary since all its materials have been configured to be physically accurate. When using materials in KeyShot, each time a new material is applied to our model, it will show up at the bottom of our material's property window. This is to allow us to recycle a material and use it again if needed. We will discuss the material properties window in more depth in the next chapter.

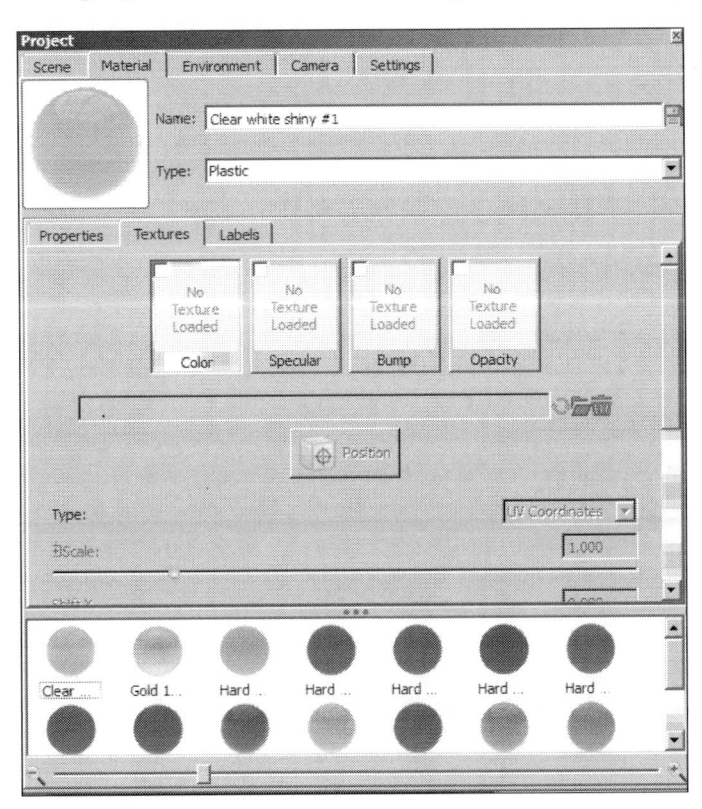

Environment

Right next to the **Material** tab we will find the **Environment** tab, which contains HDRIs that come as part of KeyShot. Here, we will be able to drag-and-drop HDRIs as well as backplates onto our scene. The **Environment** tab, just like the **Material** tab, has its own property window, which has more advanced attributes that let us assume greater control of the appearance of our scene. In the Pro version of KeyShot, an HDRI editor preference is also available for further control of our HDRIs. Certain features allow us to control the saturation, hue, brightness, contrast, and even the shape of the HDRI.

Environment properties window

The environment's properties window houses the entire list of attributes that allow us to control the lighting of our scene. We will discuss this property window in more depth in the lighting section later in this book. To access the property window, perform the following steps:

1. Double-click on any part of our model.
2. Select the **Environment** tab from the property window, as follows:

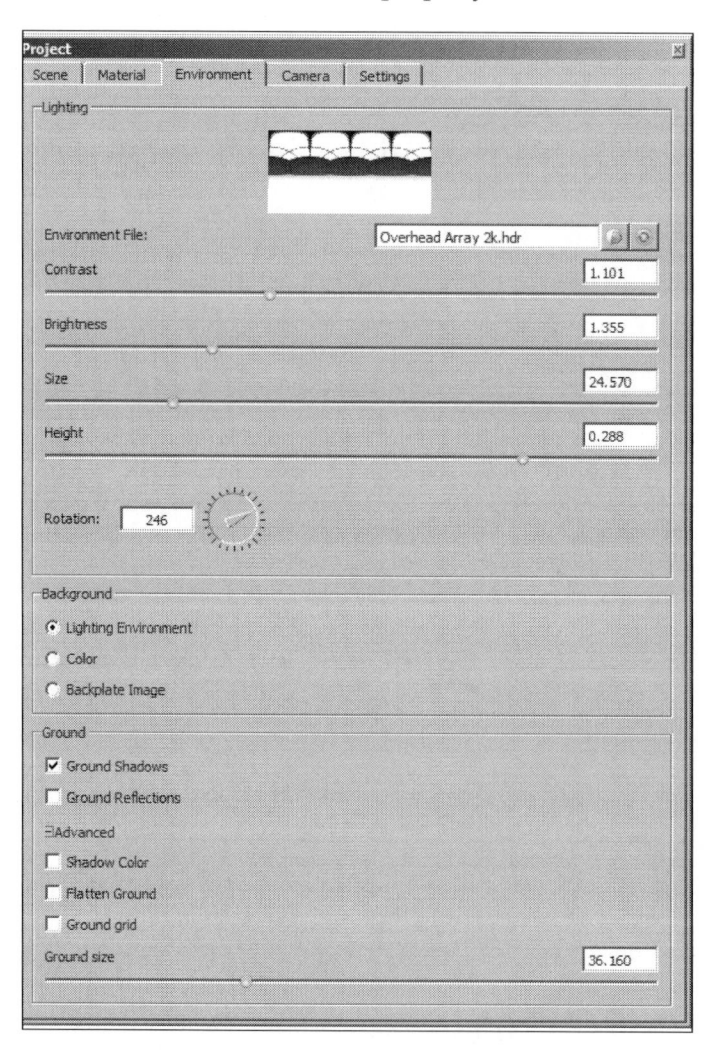

Summary

In this chapter, we have learned how to import our models into KeyShot by clicking on the Import tab from the main viewport, and we have also taken a look at creating material template, which is a newly added feature of KeyShot 3. We have also gone briefly over the three major tabs that can be found in the Project window, which are the Scene, Material, and Environment tabs. Lastly, we mentioned during the chapter that there is also a separate material properties window and a properties environment window, both of which are in charge of controlling the look of our materials and lighting.

Now that we have an understanding of how our workspace is structured and we have learned how to bring models into our scene, we will discuss in the next chapter how to apply materials and textures. We will review what each parameter does and how it differs from other traditional rendering applications.

2
Understanding Materials and Textures

Now we will learn how to set up and assign materials and how to apply textures to them to create a hyperrealistic look in our models.

In this chapter you will learn:

- Assigning and editing our materials for our project
- Understanding the materials' properties
- Creating our own unique materials
- Texturing methods

> **Downloading the example code**
> You can download the example code files for all Packt books you have purchased from your account at http://www.PacktPub.com. If you purchased this book elsewhere, you can visit http://www.PacktPub.com/support and register to have the files e-mailed directly to you.

Placing and editing materials

Continuing with our example from the previous chapter, after naming all the parts of the model, our Wacom tablet model is now ready to have materials assigned to it.

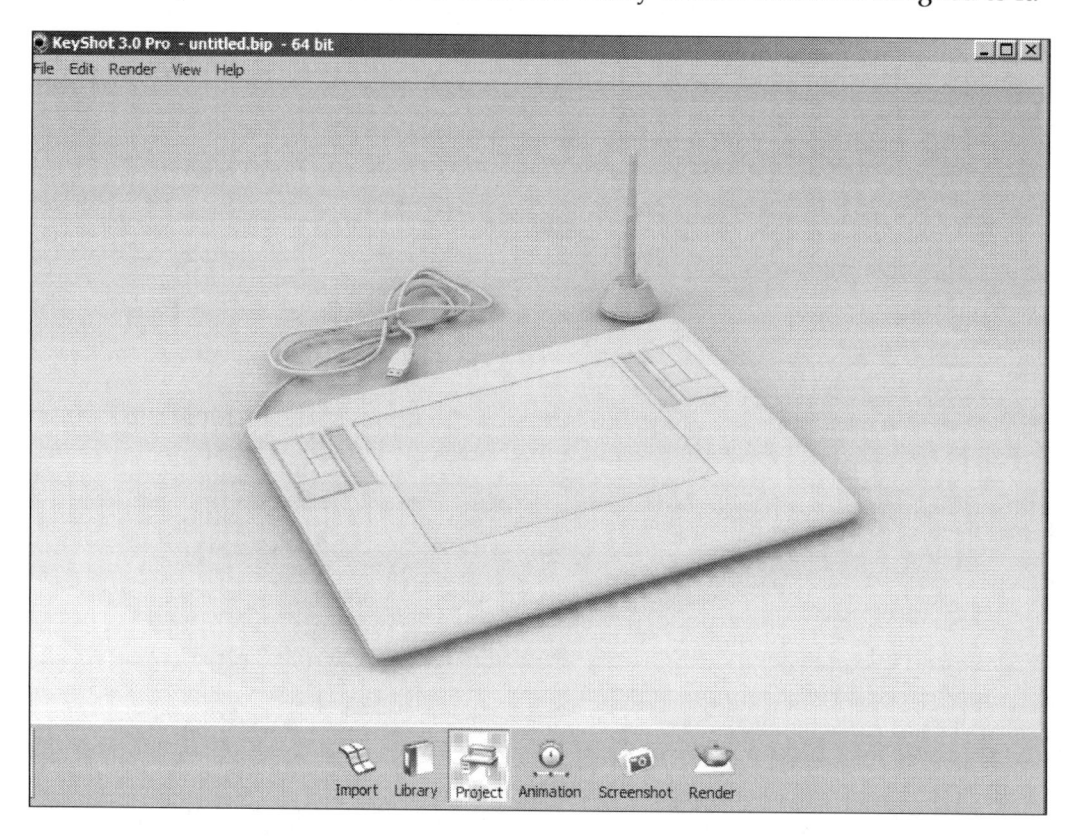

Pad

Start by adding a material to our writing pad. Perform the following steps:

1. Let's start by clicking on the **Library** icon in our viewport.
2. Select the material **Hard rough plastic – slate grey** from the plastics material folder **Plastic | Hard | Rough | Classic**.
3. Drag the material from our project window and drop it onto the pad's writing area of our Wacom tablet.
4. Double-click on the pad to open the project editor.
5. On the **Roughness** parameter let's make the value `0.120`.

6. Click on the color swatch from the diffuse channel and change the values for the following parameters:
    - **Hue**: 240
    - **Saturation**: 19
    - **Value**: 52
    - **Red**: 48
    - **Green**: 48
    - **Blue**: 52

This results in the following screenshot:

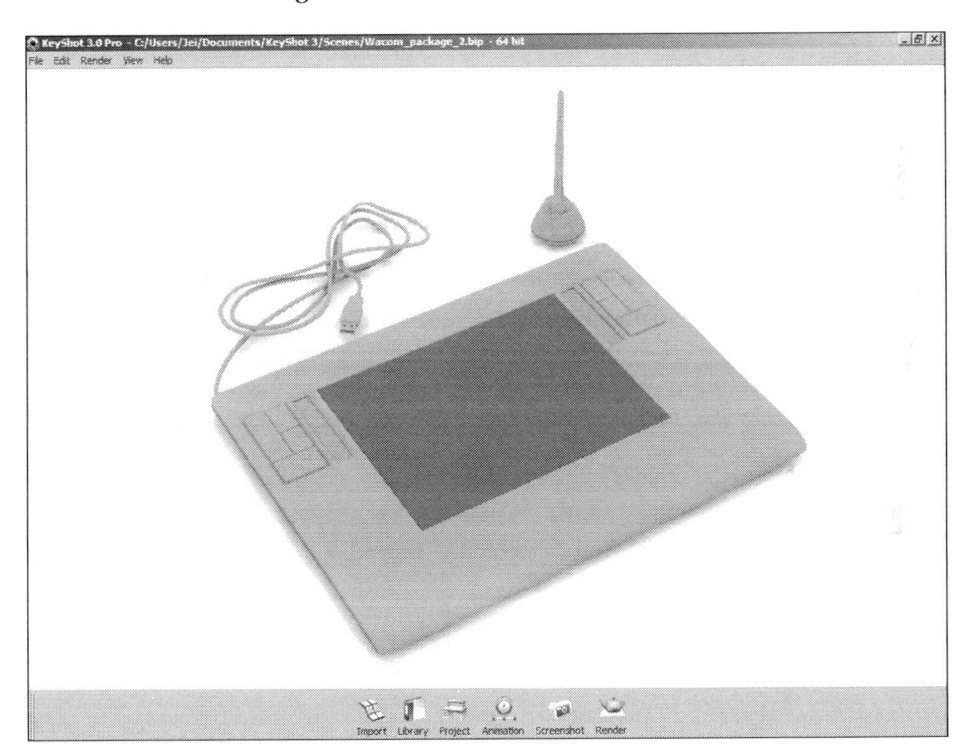

Tablet case

Under the transparent protective cover and the writing pad of the tablet, we have the case. It houses all the electronic components of our tablet, and it is made up of two similar materials. The surface of the tablet is made out of a smooth plastic material that is highly reflective, while the rest of the tablet is fit into a case also made out of plastic but with a low reflection.

Before we start assigning materials to our tablet, let's first hide the protective cover and the writing pad. Perform the following steps to do so:

1. Let's right-click on the plastic cover and select **Hide Part**.
2. Also do the same for the writing pad.
3. Let's open the **Library** window and find the **Hard rough plastic – slate grey** material by going to **Plastic | Hard | Rough | Classic**.
4. Drag the material and drop it onto the surface.
5. Click on the color swatch and change the values for the following parameters:
    - **Hue**: 240
    - **Saturation**: 16
    - **Value**: 47
    - **Red**: 44
    - **Green**: 44
    - **Blue**: 47

Buttons

Next let's work on the tablet's button, and perform the following steps:

1. Once more, drag the slate grey plastic to apply the same material to the buttons.
2. Double-click on the buttons to open the **Material Editor** window.
3. Open the color swatch again and set the values for the following parameters:
    - **Hue**: 0
    - **Saturation**: 0
    - **Value**: 30
    - **Red**: 30
    - **Green**: 30
    - **Blue**: 30

This results in the following screenshot:

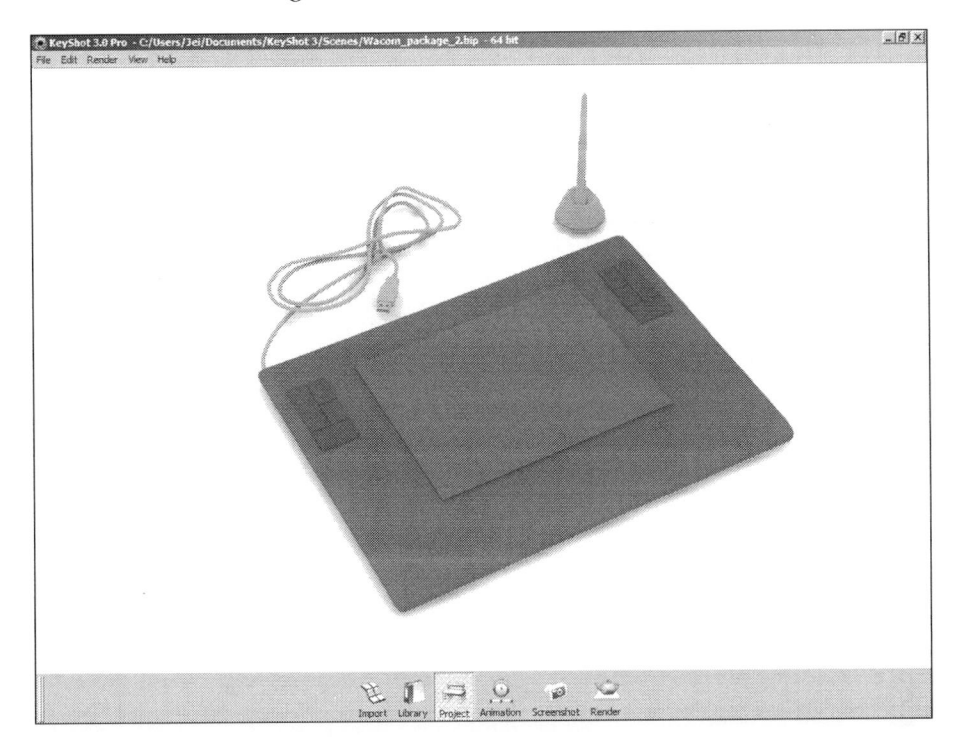

Now let's assign a material to the case that covers the sides and the bottom surface of the tablet. Perform the following steps to do so:

1. Right-click on the surface and select **Hide Part** to hide the surface of the tablet so we can work with the case.
2. With our **Library** still open let's find the **Hard rough plastic – bright amb** material in the plastic folder **Plastic | Hard | Rough | Warm**.
3. Drag-and-drop the material to our case.
4. Open the color swatch and let's set the values for the following parameters:
    - **Hue**: 57
    - **Saturation**: 56
    - **Val**: 126
    - **Red**: 126
    - **Green**: 125
    - **Blue**: 98

This results in the following screenshot:

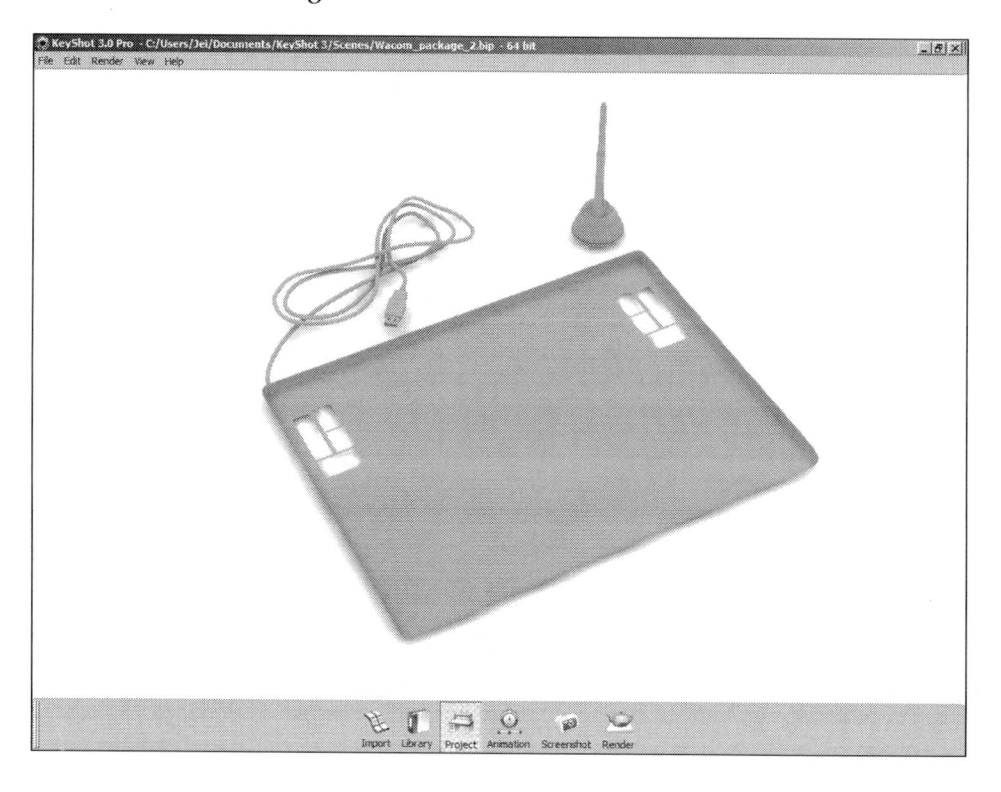

Transparent cover

For our protective cover, we will first need to unhide all our parts in the scene first, so when we go and apply the transparent material, we can see how the surface of the tablet looks through it. There are three ways to unhide parts, and they are as follows:

- The quickest way to restore all the hidden parts of our model is by hitting the right mouse button and selecting the **Show All Parts** option.
- Alternatively, we can use **Project Editor** by double-clicking on any visible part of the scene. This is done by right-clicking onto any part of the scene and selecting **Show Part in Scene Tree**.
- Once the **Project Editor** window is open, go to the **Scene** tab and select the protective cover piece and check the checkbox next to the part to unhide it from the scene.

Now, to apply a transparent material to our cover, let's perform the following steps:

1. For our cover let's use a clear plastic with high reflections.
2. Let's open our **Library** and find the **Clear white shiny** material by going to **Plastic | Clear | Shiny | Basic**.
3. Drag-and-drop the material onto our cover, which will produce the following screenshot:

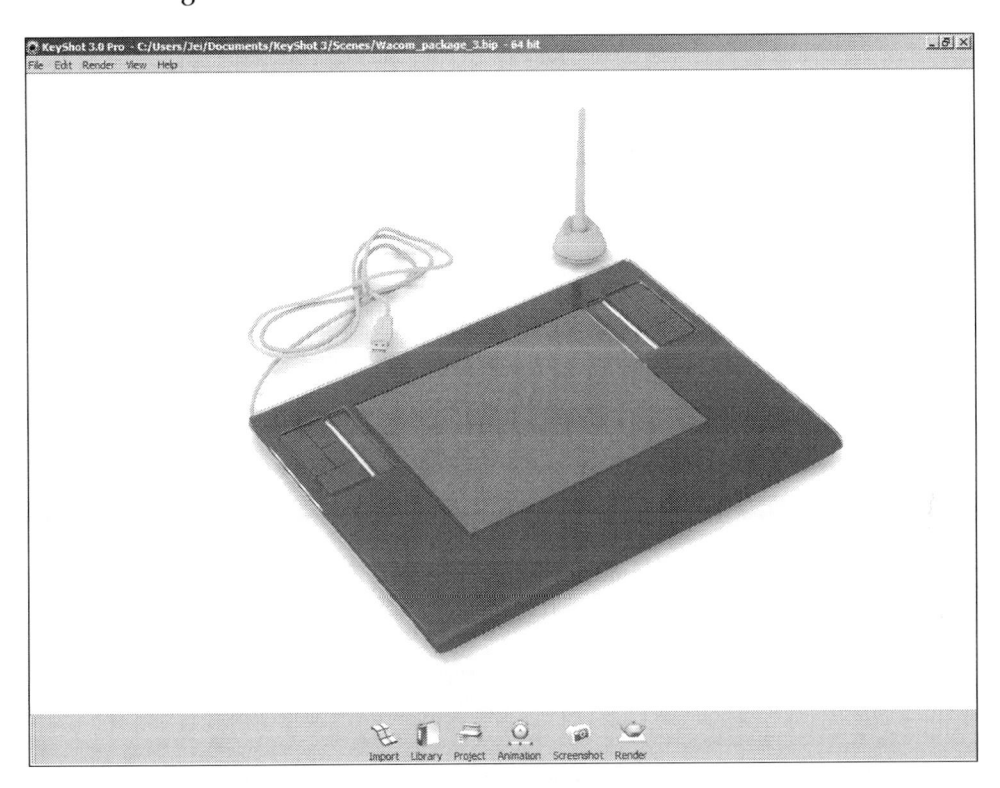

Our current scene is using the default lighting setup that comes with KeyShot. This will be a good opportunity for us to do a render of the scene and see if the lighting and the materials are working correctly. KeyShot uses **high dynamic range imaging (HDRI)** as the primary source of lighting, so it is important to pick the correct HDRI for our needs. First, let's render our scene and see how it looks. Perform the following steps to do so:

1. Click on the **Render** tab from our main viewport.

Understanding Materials and Textures

2. For our preferences, the project has been currently set up as the following:
   - Still image
   - **Format**: PNG
   - **Resolution**: 1024 x 664
   - 150 DPI

3. Click on **Render**, which produces the following screenshot:

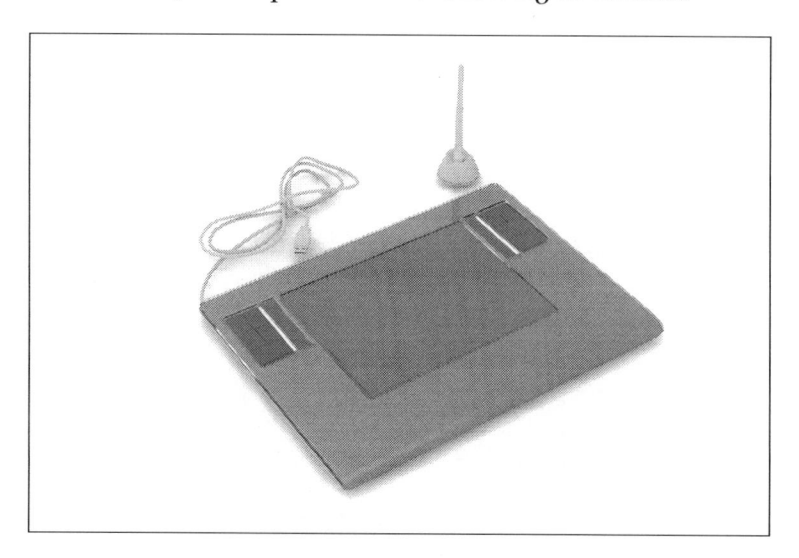

Depending on the capacity of your computer, some of the settings such as resolution and DPI may need to be lowered to increase performance. For this test, we took 15 seconds to render this image and we can see that the tablet lacks any kind of reflections or highlights in most areas. The cause for the lack of highlights and reflection is the type of HDRI we are currently using. The startup HDRI is a lighting setup used similar to that in a photo studio and it is the default lighting setup in KeyShot. For our project, however, we will need to change our lighting from the default preferences, so that we get better results when rendering our project.

Let's go ahead and change our lighting. Perform the following steps to do so:

1. Open the **Library** window from our main viewport.
2. Select the **Environment** tab from the top.
3. Find the file **Overhead Array 2k** from **Environments | Studio | Panels | Overhead**.
4. Drag-and-drop **Overheard Array 2k** onto our scene.

5. Now our scene is using a different lighting setup. From here, let's do another render test.
6. Go back to our main viewport and click on the **Render** icon. Our settings should be the same as the settings from our previous render; go ahead and click on **Render**. And here is the result of our new test:

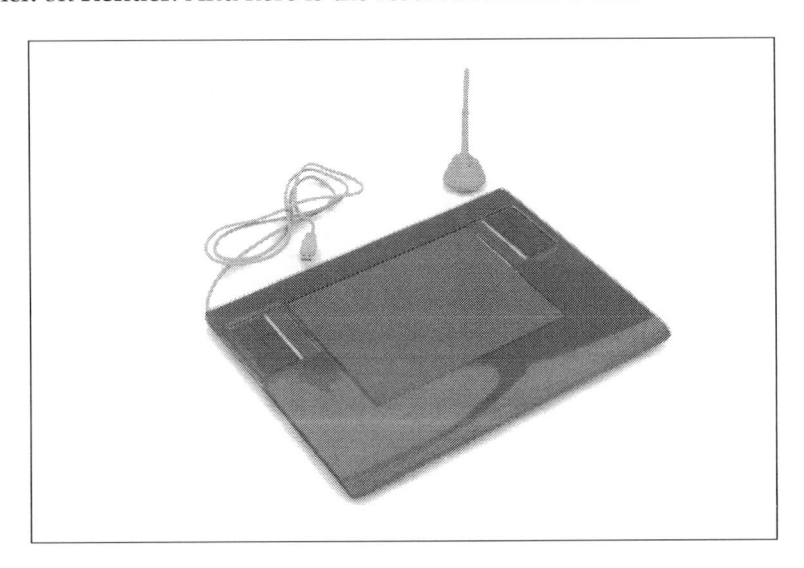

Now we can see reflections in our tablet and the highlights are no longer scattered. Since the preview we see in our main viewport is only an approximation of how our scene will look once it is finally rendered, it is always good practice to do some render tests while we are working on our scene. This will help us make any necessary corrections ahead of time.

Up to this point we have not made any significant alterations to the applied materials of our tablet nor the lighting setup. This shows how fast and easy it can be to have our projects ready for presentation in a short period of time.

Now that we have learned how to apply materials to our tablet, let's proceed by adding our Wacom logo to the tablet and applying materials to the USB cable and the Wacom pen.

Adding a label

Our tablet is now looking closer to our goal. However, in order to complete our tablet, we still need to add our Wacom logo.

Understanding Materials and Textures

Let's first hide the transparent cover. Perform the following steps to do so:

1. Double-click on the surface of the tablet.
2. Go to the **Material** tab and select **Labels**.
3. On the right-hand side of the **Labels** menu click on the **+** (plus) symbol.
4. Go to our folder by selecting **Lessons | Images**.
5. Select the **Wacom.png** file and click on **OK**.
6. Now in the **Labels** menu click on **Position Box**.
7. Place the logo below and near the center of the writing pad.
8. Use the **Angle** slide bar to rotate, and the scale to adjust the logo's size, as shown in the following screenshot:

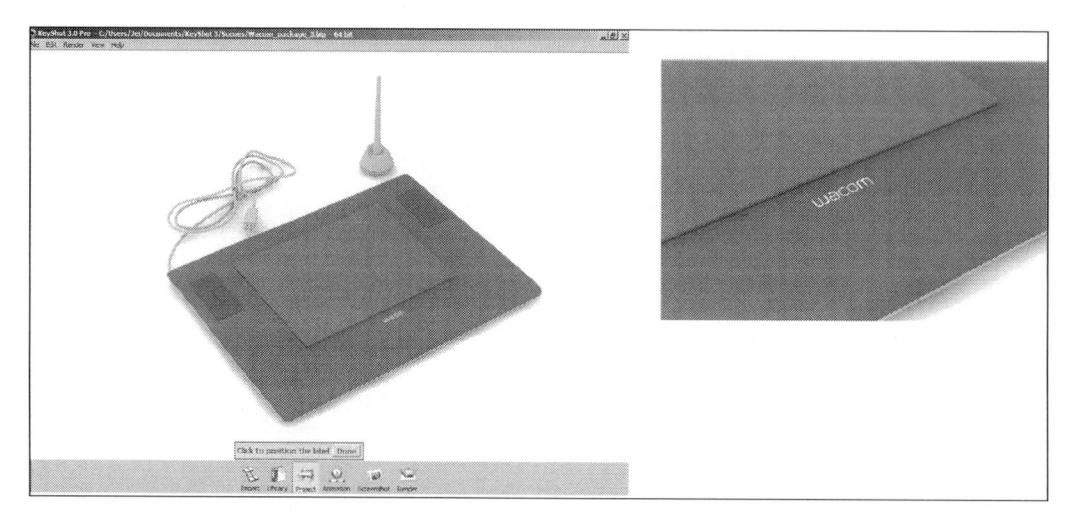

USB cable

Using the same procedure as in the previous examples, let's first zoom into the USB cable, so we can work more closely:

1. Let's zoom in by holding the *Alt* key, and right-clicking and moving the mouse backwards. To move the scene, hold the middle button of the mouse and move it until the scene is approximately centered on our screen.
2. Open the **Library** window from our viewport.
3. Go to the **Material** tab and find the material **Hard shiny plastic – grey** by selecting **Plastic | Hard | Shiny | Classic**.
4. Drag-and-drop the material onto our cable.

5. Double-click on our USB cable.
6. Open the color swatch and change the following values:
   - **Hue**: 240
   - **Saturation**: 17
   - **Value**: 43
   - **Red**: 40
   - **Green**: 40
   - **Blue**: 43

Let's repeat the same procedure for the USB case. Perform the following steps to do so:

1. Open **Library** from our viewport.
2. Go to the **Material** Tab and find the material, **Hard rough plastic – dark grey** by selecting **Plastic | Hard | Shiny | Basic**.
3. Open the color swatch and change the following values:
   - **Hue**: 0
   - **Saturation**: 0
   - **Value**: 43
   - **Red**: 43
   - **Green**: 43
   - **Blue**: 43

And again we proceed in the same way for the USB connector and the plastic holder:

1. Go to the **Material** tab and this time we will use **Gold 14k matte** by going to **Metals | Precious | Gold | Basic | Gold 14k matte**.
2. Set **Roughness** to 0.100 and **samples** to 9.
3. Drag-and-drop it onto the connector.
4. Open the color swatch and change the following values:
   - **Hue**: 43
   - **Saturation**: 213
   - **Value**: 179
   - **Red**: 179
   - **Green**: 137
   - **Blue**: 30

Understanding Materials and Textures

5. Lastly, go to the **Material** tab again.
6. Find the material, **Plastic Hard white rough** by selecting **Plastic | Hard | Rough | Basic | Hard white rough**.
7. Drag-and-drop the material on the plastic holder inside the USB connector, which will produce the following screenshots:

We have, so far, textured and applied materials to our tablet. Next we are going to focus our attention on the stylus. We are going to use the same procedure to apply materials and it is recommended, as we make progress, that we regularly check our references and compare them with our model.

Wacom stylus

We will now focus on the last object of our model. We will be applying materials the same way as we did for our tablet. At this point, we should have a fair understanding of how to assign and edit some of the materials inside KeyShot. In the following diagram, we will notice that the materials we need to apply for the stylus are the same kind of materials we used for our tablet:

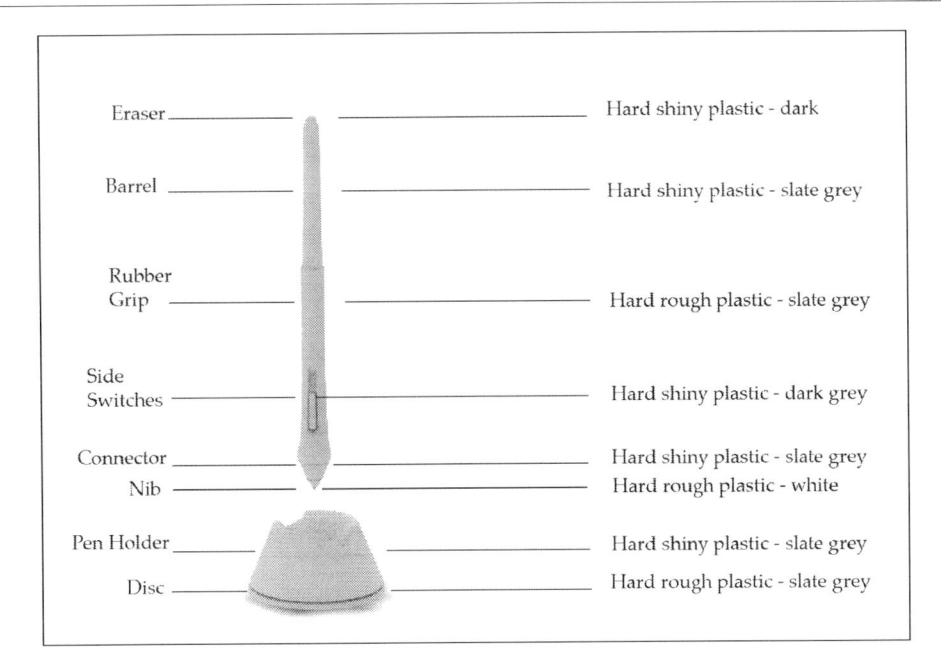

Eraser	Hard shiny plastic - dark
Barrel	Hard shiny plastic - slate grey
Rubber Grip	Hard rough plastic - slate grey
Side Switches	Hard shiny plastic - dark grey
Connector	Hard shiny plastic - slate grey
Nib	Hard rough plastic - white
Pen Holder	Hard shiny plastic - slate grey
Disc	Hard rough plastic - slate grey

Let's get started with our stylus.

Eraser

Perform the following steps to apply a material to the eraser:

1. Open **Library** from our viewport.
2. Go to the **Material** tab and search for **Hard shiny plastic – dark grey** by selecting **Plastic | Hard | Shiny | Classic**.
3. Open the color swatch and change the following values:
    - **Hue**: 210
    - **Saturation**: 11
    - **Value**: 43
    - **Red**: 42
    - **Green**: 43
    - **Blue**: 44

Barrel

Perform the following steps to apply a material to the barrel:

1. With **Library** still open, search for **Hard shiny plastic – slate grey** by selecting **Plastic | Hard | Shiny | Classic**.
2. Open the color swatch and change the following values:
   - **Hue**: 0
   - **Saturation**: 0
   - **Value**: 91
   - **Red**: 91
   - **Green**: 91
   - **Blue**: 91

Rubber grip

Perform the following steps to apply a material to the rubber grip:

1. Again with **Library** still open, apply the same material, **Hard rough plastic – slate grey**.
2. Open the color swatch and change the following values:
   - **Hue**: 280
   - **Saturation**: 17
   - **Value**: 43
   - **Red**: 42
   - **Green**: 40
   - **Blue**: 43

Side switches

Perform the following steps to apply a material to the slide switches:

1. Search for **Hard shiny plastic – slate grey** by going to **Plastic | Hard | Shiny | Classic**.
2. Open the color swatch and change the following values:
   - **Hue**: 210
   - **Saturation**: 11
   - **Value**: 44
   - **Red**: 42

- **Green**: 43
- **Blue**: 44

Connector

Perform the following steps to apply a material to the connector:

1. Search for **Hard shiny plastic – slate grey** by going to **Plastic | Hard | Shiny | Classic**.
2. Open the color swatch and change the following values:
   - **Hue**: 0
   - **Saturation**: 0
   - **Value**: 122
   - **Red**: 122
   - **Green**: 122
   - **Blue**: 122

Nib

Perform the following steps to apply a material to the nib:

1. Search for **Hard white rough** by going to **Plastic | Hard | Rough | Basic**.
2. Open the color swatch and change the following values:
   - **Hue**: 0
   - **Saturation**: 0
   - **Value**: 122
   - **Red**: 122
   - **Green**: 122
   - **Blue**: 122

This will produce the following screenshot, which shows the stylus with appropriate materials applied to its different parts:

Now that we understand the process of assigning, editing, and finding materials in KeyShot, it is time to talk a little more about the project window and the different properties that control the outlook of a material.

Understanding materials and their properties

If we take a look at a real-life tablet, in this case the Wacom Intuos 3, we will notice many interesting characteristics regarding the type of materials that the tablet was built with. For our tablet, we have chosen different kinds of plastic materials, and as you may have noticed, whenever you open the **Project Editor** window by double-clicking anywhere on our object, there are more properties and preferences available to us. Specifically, there are five categories, with each one having a different effect on the overall look of our scene. In this section, we are going to study the properties of the **Material** tab and its purpose. In general, each material has its own sets of properties inside KeyShot, and since we are using a hard rough plastic material, there are three major parameters, listed just after the following screenshot:

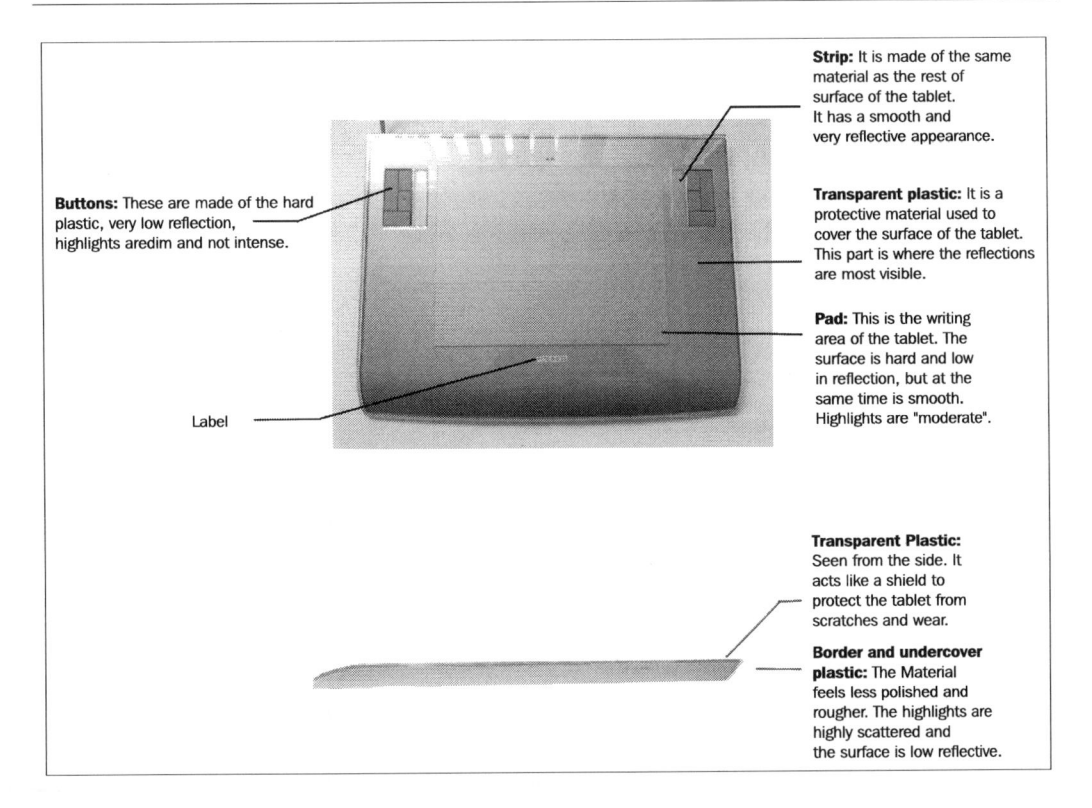

Buttons: These are made of the hard plastic, very low reflection, highlights are dim and not intense.

Label

Strip: It is made of the same material as the rest of surface of the tablet. It has a smooth and very reflective appearance.

Transparent plastic: It is a protective material used to cover the surface of the tablet. This part is where the reflections are most visible.

Pad: This is the writing area of the tablet. The surface is hard and low in reflection, but at the same time is smooth. Highlights are "moderate".

Transparent Plastic: Seen from the side. It acts like a shield to protect the tablet from scratches and wear.

Border and undercover plastic: The Material feels less polished and rougher. The highlights are highly scattered and the surface is low reflective.

The following are the three major parameters:

- **Diffuse**: This modifier allows us to control the overall color of the material. Click on the color preview and it will prompt a color swatch. **Diffuse** is a parameter that we will find in many of the materials in KeyShot. In certain materials such as metals, the color of the metal will come from the **Specular** tab.

- **Specular**: This modifier controls the intensity of our highlights and in case of metals, **Specular** also controls the color. However, in certain materials such as plastic, **Specular** only affects the intensity of the highlights. To increase or decrease the intensity of the highlights, click on the color tab of the **Specular** channel and change the desired value of the swatch from fully black (no highlight) to fully white (maximum highlight intensity).

Understanding Materials and Textures

- **Roughness**: Incrementing this value diffuses the highlights and produces less sharp softer edges. On the other hand, decreasing this value produces sharper highlights, which can be ideal for surfaces that are highly reflective. This parameter simulates the smoothness and the roughness of a surface, as follows:

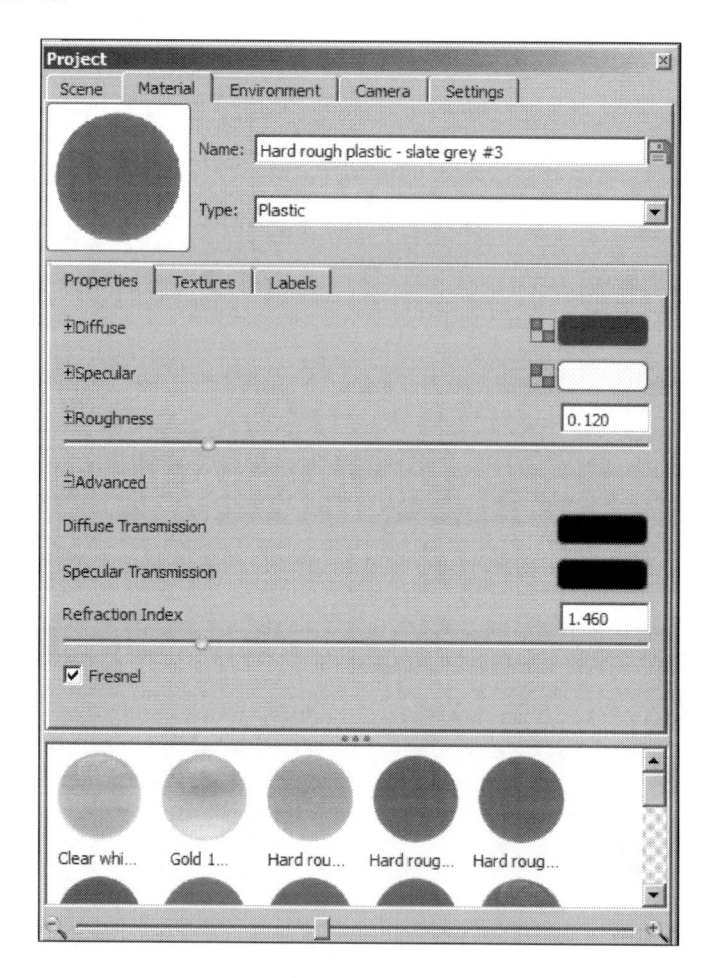

The following are the three advanced properties:

- **Diffuse Transmission**: This property can be found in the **Advanced** list of parameters of the material. **Diffuse Transmission** controls the color scattered onto a surface, which makes the material appear translucent.

- **Specular Transmission**: This is also known as transparency; raising its value to maximum white makes the material opaque, while decreasing the value to fully black makes the material transparent.

- **Refraction Index**: This is another property that we will see in other KeyShot materials. We use **Refraction Index** to indicate how much light is bent whenever it goes through a material. Each material has a different refraction index: for example, for glass the index is 1.52, while for plastic it is 1.46. Since KeyShot materials are already set up and ready to use, in most instances we won't need to use the refraction index and instead we can choose the predefined materials in KeyShot.

Texture properties

The **Textures** tab offers all channels where traditionally the maps are loaded onto in other applications. However, KeyShot is a lot more simplified and offers only the necessary properties, so that users can focus on the creative side of the project and worry less about the technical details. The following are the features:

- **Position**: Once the texture is loaded, this feature allows us to move the texture freely through the model by holding the left mouse button and dragging. It is often used when we need to place labels or decals onto the model.
- **Type**: This refers to the mapping method that the material is currently using to texture the object. KeyShot can provide different mapping methods depending on our needs. The following is a brief explanation on how each of them works:
    - **Planar X**: Choosing this method, KeyShot will project a texture on the x axis only. This is useful if we are working with an object that only needs texture projection on one side, for example a plane. In the case of a box, we project the texture only in the x axis, and the stretching will occur, as shown in the following example:

Understanding Materials and Textures

- **Planar Y**: Similar to Planar X, choosing this method, KeyShot will project a texture on the y axis only. In the Planar Y mapping method, stretching goes downwards, since there is no mapping on the other axis, shown as follows:

- **Planar Z**: Choosing this method, KeyShot will project a texture on the z axis only. When using Planar Z, the texture is stretched sideways, shown as follows:

- **Box mapping**: By choosing this method, KeyShot will now create six projections of the texture from all sides (left, right, front, and back), which includes top and bottom as well. This is the preferred mapping method for most cases, since it produces minimum stretching of the texture. When using Box mapping, all sides are mapped with minimum stretching, as follows:

- **Spherical mapping**: KeyShot uses a sphere in which the texture is projected inwards and wraps around the object. The texture's quality is at its best at the equator, as it converges towards the top and the bottom of the sphere. Spherical mapping can be used to map objects such as balls, fruits, or elongated objects such as bullets:

Understanding Materials and Textures

- **Cylindrical mapping**: This works exactly as the Spherical mapping method; however, the texture is projected through a cylinder and this mapping method is often used for objects such as tubes or pipes:

- **UV coordinates**: By choosing this method, KeyShot will try to apply a material and textures to an object if it has been UV mapped. This process of mapping will be explained more in detail in the *Texturing Materials and Methods* section of this chapter.

- **Scale**: This adjusts the size of the texture; setting this to high values produces a magnifying effect on the texture.
- **Shift X**: Decreasing or increasing this value moves the texture's position along the x coordinate.
- **Shift Y**: Decreasing or increasing this value moves the texture's position along the y coordinate.
- **Color**: The color box allows us to load a color or texture map onto the material and is commonly referred to as the diffuse channel in other applications. Depending on our needs, KeyShot provides a library of tileable textures based on photographs taken from real materials. The use of photographs enhances the quality and creates the hyperrealistic look we want in the model.
- **Specular**: The specular box acts in the same way as the reflection or highlight channel in other 3D applications. We will use this channel to upload specular maps that are made of black and white values to indicate the level of intensity of our highlights. Fully white areas in our map will give maximum highlight intensity, whereas fully black areas will render with no highlight intensity.

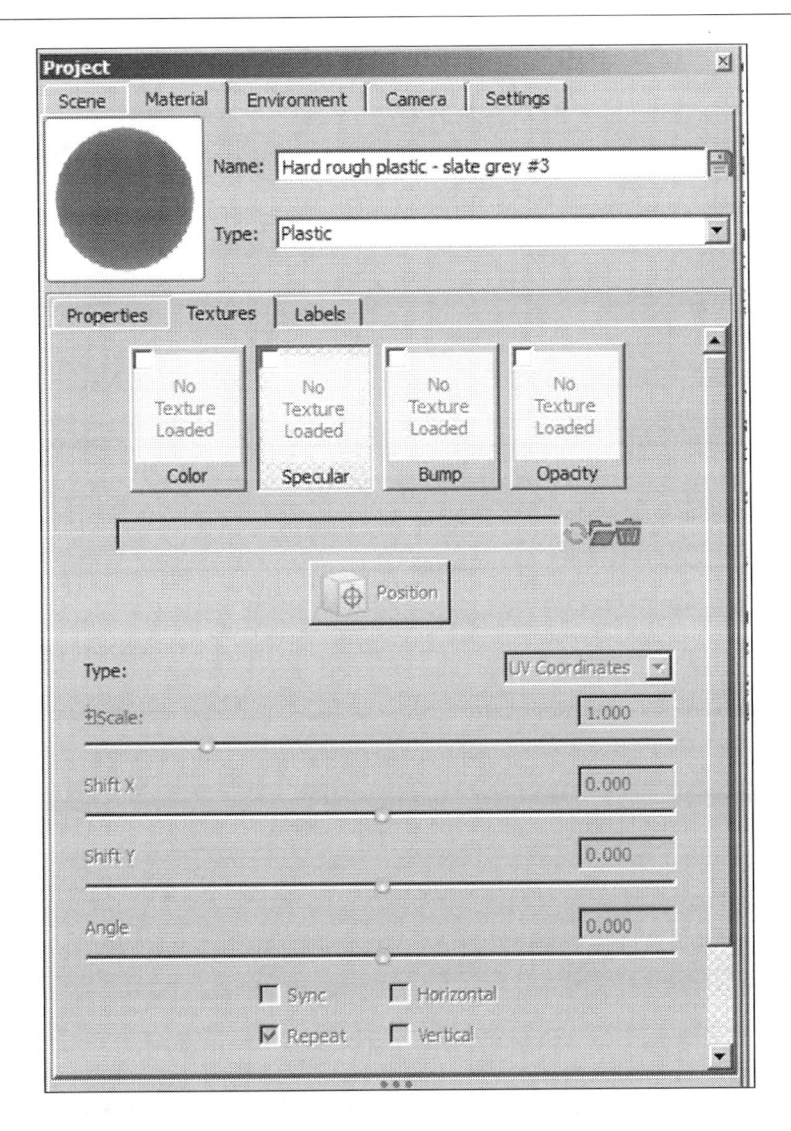

- **Bump**: The bump channel allows us to load our bump maps or normal maps to enhance the level of realism of our materials. A brief explanation of the two maps is given as follows:
    - **Bump maps**: These are created using black and white values to simulate raised or depressed areas. It simulates depressions in those areas where the map is dark, while areas that are white simulate raised parts of the texture.

- ○ **Normal maps**: These are similar to bump maps, but have more colors, which allows for more complex effects than only black and white. Normal maps are composed of **Red Green Blue (RGB)** information that corresponds to the X, Y, and Z coordinates of a surface's normal.
- **Opacity**: The opacity channel allows us to upload maps with transparency or to add transparency to maps that don't have an alpha channel embedded in the image. For this, there are three different methods for creating opacity maps, as follows:
    - ○ **Images with transparency**: These are images that have an embedded alpha channel.
    - ○ **Colored images**: KeyShot will automatically interpret the values of the white and black areas of an image and produce transparency accordingly. Areas of an image that are 100 percent black are considered fully transparent, while areas that are gray or 50 percent black and white are considered half transparent.
    - ○ **Inverse**: Using this method KeyShot will treat areas that are white as transparent, and dark or black areas as opaque.
- **Sync**: When this property is checked, it synchronizes all the textures that are being used, so when modifications are being made such as scaling, all textures are modified simultaneously. It is always recommended to keep this property checked when working with textures.

Labels tab

Labels are images such as logos, symbols, or decals that work in a similar way as stickers in real life. For an easier placement, sometimes decals or logos are better placed if they are not part of the texture (an example would be when the model is UV mapped). The **Labels** property tab is similar to the **Textures** tab. It contains the same parameters that allow us to move, scale, and position the image over the model, but there are some additional properties, shown as follows:

- **Intensity**: This controls the brightness of the label using white as 100 percent intensity.
- **Depth**: This parameter measures how far a label is projected into the texture.
- **IOR**: This is also known as the index of refraction. In the case of labels, **IOR** works as a transparency parameter. It is mostly used to control the reflection on labels.
- **Specular**: Changing the **Specular** property allows us to control the highlight of the label.

- **Two sided**: When this checkbox is checked, KeyShot will make the label appear visible from the front and back, for example when we place a logo on a transparent material such as a plastic or a glass. Check the **Two sided** checkbox to make the logo visible through the back of the glass.

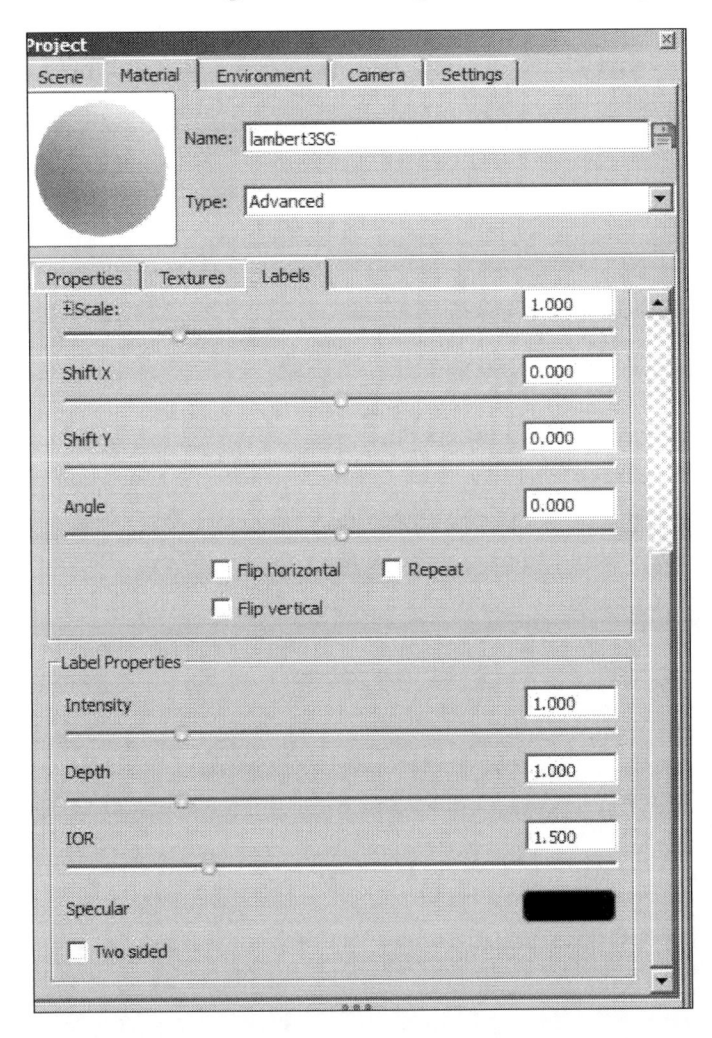

So far, we have learned how to assign materials, and the flexibility and variety of controls that the project window offers to us to edit those materials. Understanding the project window and its properties is important, because it allows us not only to modify the look of an existing material, but using it with what we have learned, we can also create our own materials.

Understanding Materials and Textures

Next we are going to take a look at how we can create materials. Although KeyShot offers a huge library of materials, there will be occasions when we need to modify those materials or even create our own to use them for our own project.

How to create materials

We can begin creating a new material in KeyShot in a number of ways. It can be based on an existing material in the library or we can create it from scratch. The following methods will help us understand the possibilities as well as the limitations of some of the materials we use. I also encourage everyone to experiment with different ways of creating the materials on their own.

Whenever we first open KeyShot and import one of our objects into our scene, by default the type of material that is applied to the object is the advanced type, which is a generic material that basically can be used to recreate other types of materials.

The list of the type of materials in KeyShot can be found under the name of **Material** in the project window. For our purposes we will discuss a few different types of materials that are often used and also the advantages and limitations of each one of them.

These materials are listed in the following section.

Plastics

As we learned previously from our Wacom tablet exercise, plastic is a material that can be found almost anywhere, from daily appliances to computer components. As it is a very common material, most of the time we will be using plastics in our projects. To understand how plastics work, let's start by creating a new project. Perform the following steps to do so:

1. Click on **File** and select **New...**.
2. Let's go and import our `Sphere.obj` file into our scene by going to **Lesson | Keyshot_models | data**.
3. Double-click on the sphere and change the material type by setting **Type** to **Plastics**.
4. Open **Library** from our viewport and in the **Environment** tab, drag-and-drop onto the scene our **Overhead Array 2k HDRI** map.

Now in KeyShot, some materials have the ability to be modified and appear as another type of material. Depending on the kind of look we are trying to achieve, for example, a plastic material can be modified to appear as a piece of glass. However, the same cannot be achieved by using a glass material to make it look like a plastic. This is because a glass material type has limited options in terms of editing.

Creating glass using plastic

Perform the following steps to create glass using plastic:

1. With the project window open, let's click on the **Specular** channel and bump up the value to **180,** or we can raise it up by moving up the slider on the side. This will give our sphere a little bit of highlight.

    Since our goal is to try to recreate a transparent plastic that can be found anywhere else under normal lighting conditions, it is recommended to leave the specular color within the range of black and white scale. Changing the specular color may cause our highlights to look unrealistic.

2. Set the **Diffuse** color to black.
3. Set **Roughness** to 0.
4. Next, we are going to increase the value for the **Specular** transmission to **250**, which controls the transparency of our plastic and also lets us pick a color. In in this case, I chose a bright yellow color.

As we can see, the color applied to the **Specular Transmission** channel makes our plastic look yellow, and at the same time, as **Roughness** is set to 0 and the **Diffuse** color is set to black, our plastic resembles a glass material.

However, if our goal was to create a cloudy semi-transparent plastic, all we have to do is lower **Specular Transmission** and increase the diffuse intensity, so our plastic looks a little less transparent.

Another interesting experiment we can try is to increase the **Refraction Index** value and lower our **Specular Transmission** to 0. Now our plastic is not transparent anymore, but our reflections are a lot sharper, which makes our material resemble a metal more than a plastic.

Understanding Materials and Textures

Once we start applying textures to our plastic, we can create a new range of materials such as concrete, wood, and even metal panels. This is possible because plastic materials have properties such as **Diffuse Transmission** and **Specular Transmission**, which allow us to have more control over the look of the material. The following screenshots show some glass material looks created using plastic, cloudy semi-transparent plastic, and reflective plastic, respectively:

Metals

Unlike plastics, metals do not have advanced properties such as **Diffuse Transmission**, **Specular Transmission**, or **Refraction Index**, so in order to replicate the look of other materials, metals will have to rely on textures. However, we can create a few anodized metals by simply changing the **Roughness** value. KeyShot's library of metal materials has a wide range of metal materials that we can use for most of our needs.

Glass

When we use a glass material, we will notice that in our properties tab we no longer have the diffuse and specular channels. Instead we have a color channel, which is in charge of the overall color of our glass. The reason there are fewer parameters is that we no longer need them, since KeyShot has already set up our glass material to only work as intended. However, we can create many kinds of glasses by using bump or normal maps to change the surface of the glass.

Advanced

Advanced is another type of material that can be found inside the list of the project window. What is special about the advanced material is that it can be used to create other kinds of materials such as glass, plastics, metals, and so on because it features most of the properties we need. The following are some of the examples that can be created using the advanced material along with textures provided by KeyShot. The following screenshots show a glass material with a normal texture, a metal material having an iron cast texture with a color and a bump map, and a solid material having a brick color and bump map, respectively:

Now that we know how to create materials using parameters, we are ready to create even more complex materials by learning how to upload textures onto our materials.

Texturing materials and methods

To complete our understanding of how to apply realistic materials onto our models, we will need to understand the process of applying textures. Inside KeyShot there are many ways to map an object in order to prepare it for the texturing phase. We previously mentioned the various mapping methods, as follows:

- Planar X, Y, and Z
- UV coordinates
- Box
- Spherical
- Cylindrical

By default, when we first import an object to our scene, the UV coordinates method is automatically chosen as the standard mapping solution. UV mapping is often a long and tedious process in which we take a flat 2D image and place it or texture it onto a 3D object. This method is more commonly used by professionals in the entertainment business because of the high demand in quality.

However, the preferred mapping method for most of our needs will be the Box mapping approach. Using this method we do not have to worry about UV coordinates because all the textures placed onto our models will be done through projections.

Understanding Materials and Textures

For a better understanding of how to apply textures in KeyShot using the Box mapping method, let's go ahead and start a new project. Perform the following steps to do so:

1. Select the **File** menu and choose to create a new scene.
2. Let's import a new object into our scene. Select the **Bullet.obj** file from **Lessons | keyshot_models | data**.
3. Click on **OK**.

Let's name all the pieces of our bullet so it is easier to identify which part we are working with. Also let's assign a proper material to each of the pieces using the same approach as we did for the tablet exercise.

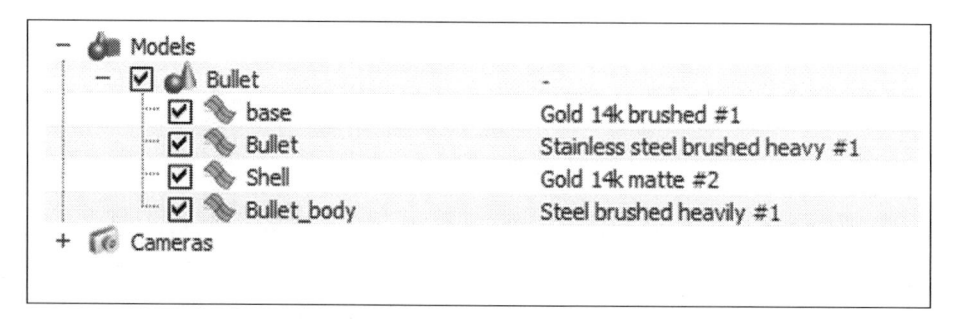

```
- Models
  - ☑ Bullet
      ☑ base              Gold 14k brushed #1
      ☑ Bullet            Stainless steel brushed heavy #1
      ☑ Shell             Gold 14k matte #2
      ☑ Bullet_body       Steel brushed heavily #1
+ Cameras
```

After naming all the pieces of our bullet and having all the materials assigned to our object, it should resemble the following photo:

We may notice the materials here. For the color property of each material, I have the following values:

[46]

- For the base of the bullet, change the following values:
    - **Hue**: 32
    - **Saturation**: 181
    - **Value**: 212
    - **Red**: 212
    - **Green**: 142
    - **Blue**: 62
- For the tip of the bullet, change the following values:
    - **Hue**: 48
    - **Saturation**: 5
    - **Value**: 224
    - **Red**: 224
    - **Green**: 223
    - **Blue**: 219
- For the body of the bullet, change the following values:
    - **Hue**: 27
    - **Saturation**: 18
    - **Value**: 152
    - **Red**: 152
    - **Green**: 146
    - **Blue**: 141
- And finally for the shell, change the following values:
    - **Hue**: 38
    - **Saturation**: 186
    - **Value**: 166
    - **Red**: 166
    - **Green**: 122
    - **Blue**: 45

Next we are going to add some textures to our bullet. Most of the materials that we are going to use are already provided by KeyShot, so I recommend experimenting with different textures and parameters to see what interesting results we might get.

Understanding Materials and Textures

For assigning textures to the base, perform the following steps:

1. Open the project window by double-clicking on the base of the bullet.
2. Go to the **Textures** tab and click on the **Bump** small box in the upper-left corner to open the browser.
3. Make sure the mapping method for the base is **UV coordinate**.
4. Go to the **Lessons** folder and find the `Bullet-NM.tif` file by going to **Lessons | Textures**.
5. Make sure our **Bump height** parameter is set to `-0.730`.
6. Also make sure the **Normal Map** checkbox is checked.

For assigning textures to the bullet, perform the following steps:

1. Double-click on the tip of the bullet.
2. Go to the **Textures** tab and click on the **Color** small box in the upper-left corner to open the browser.
3. Make sure the mapping method is **Box**.
4. Go to KeyShot's **Texture** folder at the location `C:\Users\Jei\Documents\KeyShot 3`.
5. Find the **Rust.jpg** file, select it, and click on **OK**.
6. Now repeat the same process to load `Rust_normal.jpg` under the **Bump** channel box.
7. Now let's make sure that our textures are synchronized by checking the box.
8. Change our **Scale** to `0.430`.
9. Also make sure the **Normal Map** checkbox is checked.

Next let's apply a texture to the body of our bullet. Perform the following steps to do so:

1. Since we previously applied a material with a preset texture let's go to the **Textures** tab and make sure the mapping method is **Box**.
2. Make sure that **Scale** is `0.250` and **Bump height** is `0.990`.
3. Since we are using a bump map, there is no need to check the **Normal Map** checkbox for this texture.

Lastly let's apply a texture to the shell of the bullet. Perform the following steps to do so:

1. Double-click on the shell.
2. Again go to the **Textures** tab and click on the **Bump** small box in the upper-left corner to open the browser.
3. Make sure the mapping method is **Box**.
4. Find the **Rust_normal.jpg** file, select it, and click on **OK**.
5. Leave the map as a bump. Do not check the **Normal Map** checkbox.
6. Make sure **Scale** is `0.250` and **Bump height** is `-0.160`.

We have now completed the texturing process of our bullet. As an interesting experiment, our bullet is an object that actually has been UV mapped previously. We could therefore have chosen UV coordinates as the mapping method for this exercise, but we will leave it here and experiment on it later on.

At this point, we should have acquired a basic understanding of how materials and textures are applied to our models inside KeyShot.

Summary

In this chapter, we saw that all the materials can be found by clicking on the Library icon from our viewport. To apply a material all we need to do is select the material we want from the drop-down list and drag-and-drop it onto the model. We can adjust the look of a material by double-clicking on the material and opening the properties window. We have studied the different ways we can texture and apply materials to our models. For most situations, using box mapping is the recommended method, since it gives the best results and avoids texture stretching. Box mapping is also ideal for parametric modeling software such as SolidWorks or AutoCAD. UV mapping is mostly used for models that have been mapped with UV coordinates and is often used for models from applications such as 3ds Max or Maya. Labels work as decals or stickers that can be placed onto our models by adding them to the label's tab. This images are normally exported with a transparency or alpha channel from another application such as Photoshop. In order to create our own materials we can use glass, metal, or plastic as the base material, since all three of them do not share the same material properties.

In our next chapter, we are going to take a look at how to set up our lighting in KeyShot by studying its parameters and their individual contributions to the look of our scene.

3
Lighting Made Easy

In order to create high-quality images in KeyShot, we need to understand the importance of lighting and how it works. KeyShot's method of lighting is a lot simpler than other applications, allowing us with little effort to easily set up different environments and conditions. In this chapter we will also discuss how to work with cameras and modify them for our projects.

In this chapter you will learn about:

- How to use HDRI and backplates to set our environment
- The environment tabs and their parameters
- How to configure real-time settings
- How to use cameras

Setting up our scene

So far, we have studied how materials behave once we start changing their properties to achieve different kinds of looks. Now we are going to take a look at how lighting can also influence the overall appearance of our object and the scene. KeyShot does not use traditional lighting setups such as 3ds Max, Maya, SolidWorks, or other modeling applications, so all lighting is dependent on high Hyphenate resolution, 32-bit channel HDR. This makes working in KeyShot a lot simpler and to "allows us to avoid getting tangled up with the technical aspects of the software.

To understand how lighting works inside KeyShot, let's continue with our Wacom tablet project from *Chapter 2, Understanding Materials and Textures*, or we can also load the *Chapter 2* project file from our disc, as follows:

1. Open up KeyShot.
2. From the **File** menu, select **Open**.

Lighting Made Easy

3. Find `Wacom_project_chap2.ksp` from our disc by navigating to **Lessons | Keyshot files**.
4. Select file and click on **OK**.
5. A prompt will appear asking whether we want to copy all the files to the same location or to a new folder, as shown in the following screenshot:

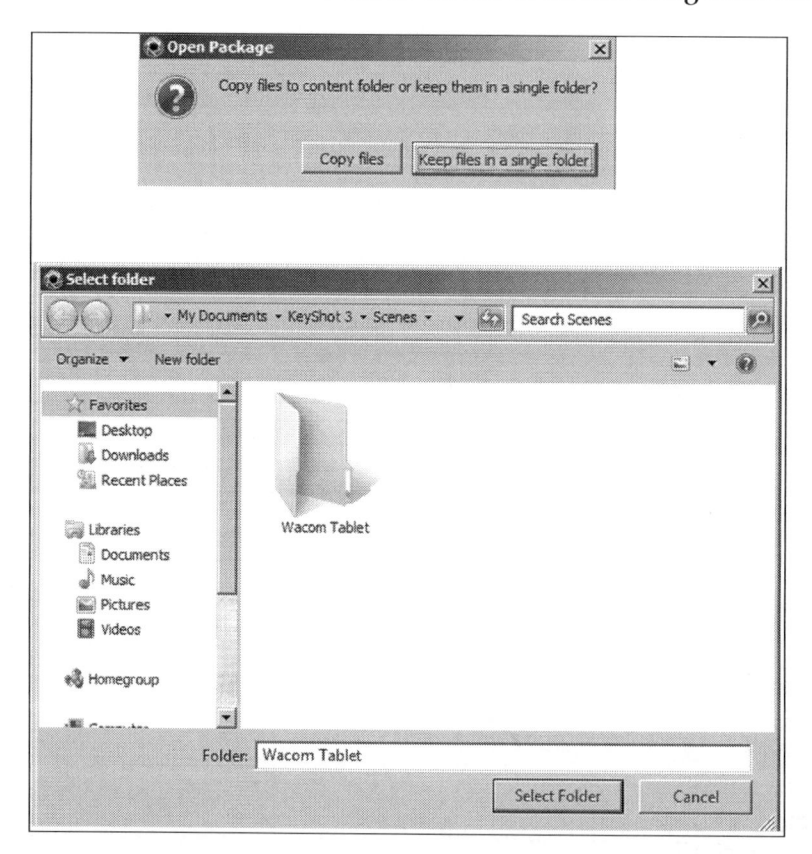

6. Select the **Keep files in single folder** option; this will open another window linked to the scene folder.
7. Right-click on the scene folder, create a new folder, and name it as `Wacom Tablet_chapter2`. Select the folder and click on **OK**.
8. KeyShot will extract all the files from `Wacom_project_chap2.ksp` into the folder.

Chapter 3

When we save our project files in KeyShot, they are generally saved in a BIP format. This file format contains the locations of textures, materials, HDRIs, and other parameters within KeyShot. However, there is another option that allows us to save our projects into a package file that contains all the textures and HDRIs, along with the BIP file of our project. These package files have the KSP extension; we would use them when we need to have all our files condensed into one file for easier organization.

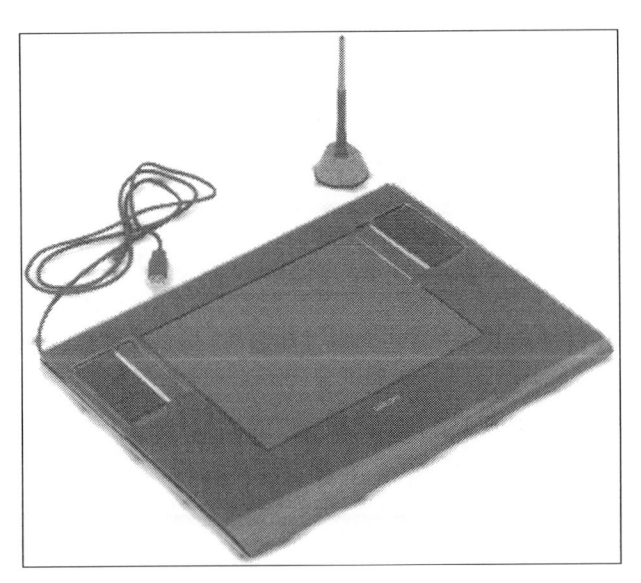

To begin with applying lighting to our scene, first we have to be sure of what the overall objective of our scene is. For example, if our objective is to design our scene for a product presentation environment, then perhaps the best choice of lighting setup would be utilizing a photo studio type of HDRI, instead of using outdoor environments. For our project we want our object to be displayed in an indoor environment, similar to a studio or an office.

Let's start by adjusting our lighting by first selecting the appropriate backplate for our scene. Perform the following steps to do so:

1. Click on the **Library** icon of our viewport.
2. Go to the **Backplates** tab.
3. Select **Interior | Office desk | office desk 50mm 3**.

Lighting Made Easy

4. Drag-and-drop the backplate onto our scene.

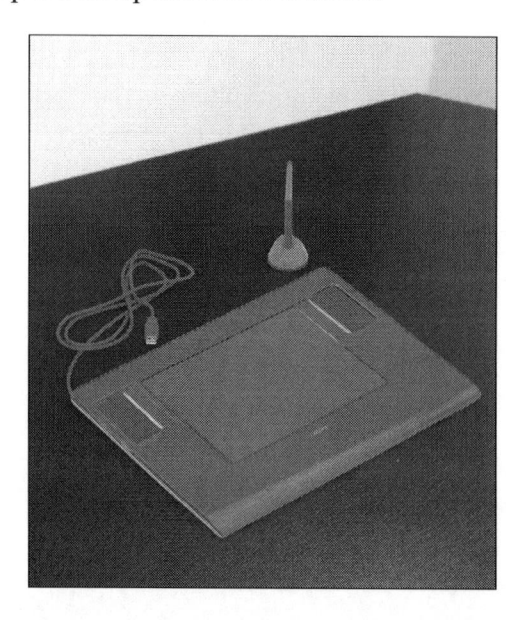

We can now see in the preceding screenshot that our backplate has been loaded onto our scene. Next, let's rotate and move our object until it is placed correctly onto the image. By looking at our scene now, we see that our object is not lit up correctly compared to the backplate. At the bottom of the image, our office desk has a strong light coming from the ceiling illuminating our table, which produces a scattered highlight that is not seen in our tablet. We can also see reflections from the wall on our desk, so in order to make our object look more convincing, we need to use the HDRI that has been created in the same environment to reproduce the lighting and all the reflections that we need on our object.

HDRIs and backplates are usually photographs that have been taken and processed together as a set so designers and artists can use them to create realistic environments. In most applications, HDRIs are used to reproduce the reflections and sometimes the lighting on an object or multiple objects, while backplates work as the background of the scene in the same way as a matte painting. We can find sets of HDRIs and backplates sold at various websites. For example, one of my favorites is http://www.hdri4u.com/; they offer a free set of HDRIs and backplates once a month and they also have great HDRI sets for sale.

Now that we have learned why HDRIs and backplates are used in conjunction, let's load an HDRI for our particular scene:

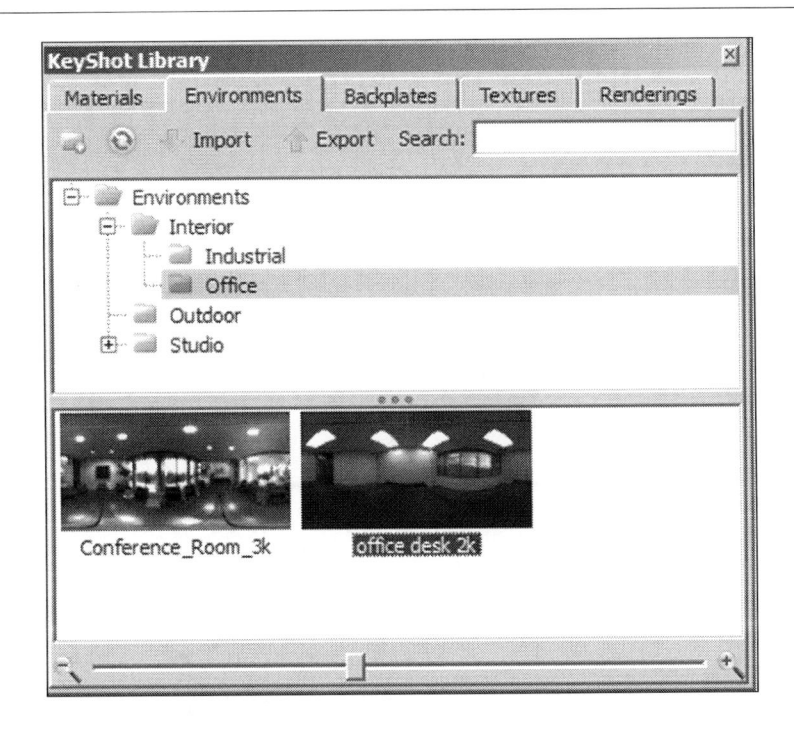

Perform the following steps:

1. Let's click on the **Library** icon from the viewport again.
2. Go to the **Environments** tab.
3. Select the **Environments** subfolder and then select **Interior | Office**.
4. Drag-and-drop the HDRI, **office desk 2k**, onto our scene.
5. Open the **Project Editor** window by double-clicking anywhere on our object or by clicking on the **Project** icon on the main viewport.
6. Go to the **Environment** tab and input the following values:
    - **Contrast**: 0.699
    - **Brightness**: 2.040
    - **Size**: 44.710
    - **Height**: 0.173
    - **Rotation**: 267
7. Scroll down our menu tab and make sure the **Ground Shadows** checkbox is checked.

Lighting Made Easy

8. Also set **Ground Size** to `6.235`.
9. Lastly, save our project and name it as `Wacom_tablet`.

After loading an HDRI, we now have reflections visible on the transparent cover of our tablet. We have configured the parameters in the **Environment** tab to make sure our object shows the shadows, highlights, and reflections that would be present in an office environment. This quick example shows how easy it is to have a scene set up and ready to render without the need to configure multiple lights.

So far, we have learned the basics of configuring the lighting inside KeyShot. Using HDRIs and backplates can really boost the quality and the look we are to after, as follows:

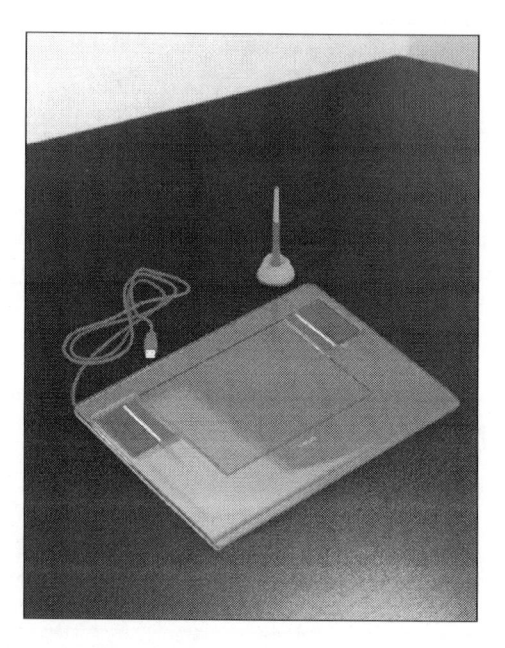

Lighting properties

One of the reasons that I use KeyShot, as one of my primary tools as an artist, is that KeyShot has an easier learning curve compared to other rendering packages. If you are currently using other applications such as Maya or 3ds Max, you may find that adjusting the lighting for a scene can be a lengthy and complex process that often requires hours of preparations. In this industry, where time is normally considered a luxury, it is essential to have the necessary tools to increase productivity without compromising quality. For this reason, I strongly recommend using KeyShot for projects such as product showcasing or visual development, because setting up the lighting is one of the easiest and most straightforward tasks.

As we have become more familiar with the different settings that KeyShot has to offer, we might have noticed from the previous chapters that the parameters in the **Environment** tab sound familiar. This is because the interface has been designed with a focus on simplicity, which allows users, regardless of their discipline, to be able to concentrate on the aesthetics of their projects without worrying about the technical aspects of the program.

The **Environment** tab is made up of three different categories; each one controls a portion of the scene in a different manner.

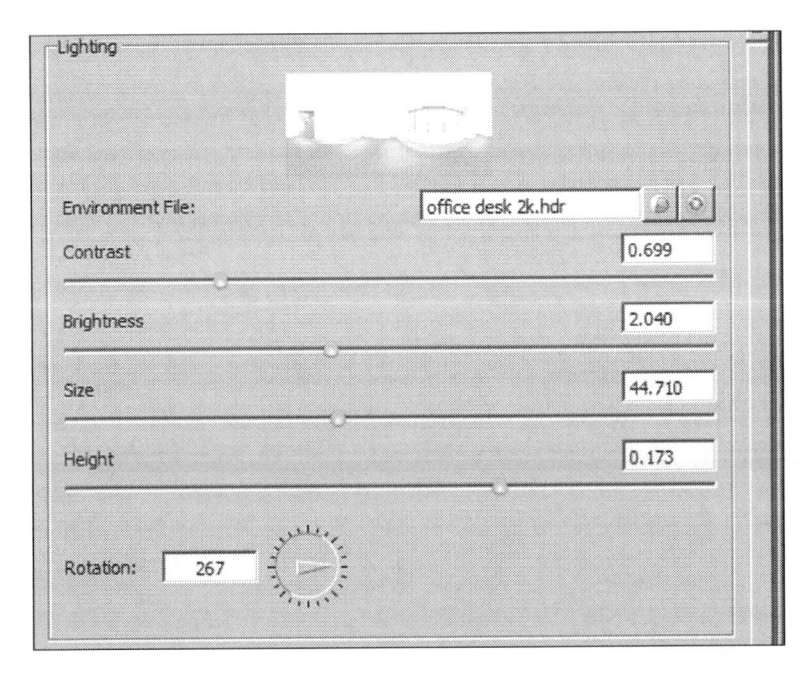

The different controls from the **Lighting** section allow us to make modifications to our HDRI file. The following are those controls:

- **Contrast**: This slider controls the difference of intensity between lit and shadowed areas cast into our scene. Raising the slider will sharpen the shadowed areas, basically creating sharper edges in our shadows, while decreasing the value will create a softer effect on the edges. Also contrast can be used to increase the sharpness of the reflections on plastic, metallic, or any reflective surfaces. KeyShot recommends leaving this at its default value, since increasing or decreasing it can produce inaccurate results.

Lighting Made Easy

- **Brightness**: This controls the overall light intensity of our HDRI file. We can increase or decrease the brightness by using the slider or by using the up and down arrow keys. Another way of controlling the brightness is through the **Brightness** and **Gamma** parameters located in the **Settings** tab, which we will discuss later in this chapter.

- **Size**: Incrementing the value of this parameter will expand our environment, creating bigger reflections and areas of shadow and light. Exactly the opposite effect will occur if we decrease the value of this slider, which will make our areas of highlights and shadows smaller, as well as the reflections.

- **Height**: This parameter will allow us to control the source of lighting on the y axis. By increasing or decreasing the value of the height, we can control the displacement of our highlights and the reflections vertically.

- **Rotation**: This is another parameter that allows us to control the displacement of our source of lighting in the scene. The rotation manifold can be used to rotate our highlights from our HDRI around the scene and is often used along with the **Height** parameter.

Next we have the **Background** section in our **Environment** tab. In this category there are three options for applying a background image to our scene.

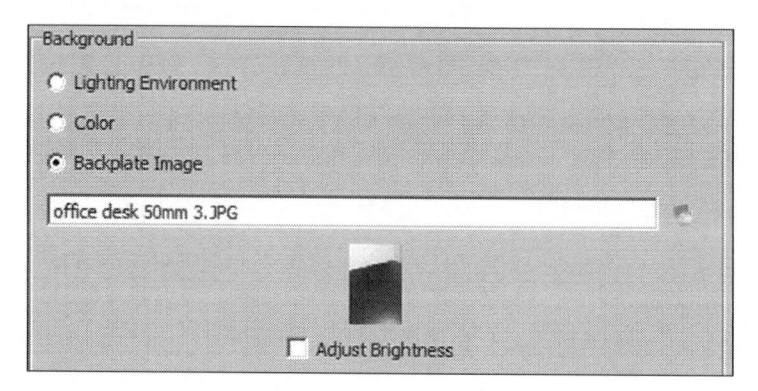

The following are those three options:

- **Lighting Environment**: By using this option, KeyShot will use the HDR image as our background image.

- **Color**: This option will allow us to pick a solid color and use it as a background instead of an image file.

- **Backplate Image**: As the name implies, this lets us pick an image, usually a photograph file that comes along with an HDRI set of our choice, to use as a background.

The last section of the **Environment** tab is the **Ground** section. By default, when our objects are loaded into KeyShot, they rest on an invisible surface. We can use this surface to represent the ground or floor for our models.

If we want to cast shadows onto the floor by a light source behind our object, we can do so by checking the **Ground Shadows** checkbox. If our object is resting on a polished surface and we want reflections instead, we can check the **Ground Reflections** checkbox. The following are the controls in the **Ground** section:

- **Shadow Color**: This allows us to control the color of our shadows. It is recommended to leave this checkbox unchecked in most cases, since changing the color can create inconsistencies in the look of our shadows.
- **Flatten Ground**: This projects our object onto a flat surface.
- **Ground Grid**: This creates a Cartesian grid on the floor. This is useful at times when we need to measure distances between objects or adjust the perspective of a model to match our background image.
- **Ground Size**: This parameter controls the resolution of our surface or ground. Increasing its value stretches our ground plane, which in turn reduces the number of pixels, which may cause the shadows of our object to look blocky. Decreasing the value of this parameter reduces the size of our ground plane and increases the number of pixels. This parameter is often left at low values to create realistic shadows and reflections.

In the next example we can see the effects of the shadows and reflections projected onto the ground when having the ground shadows and ground reflections turned on. Also, for a better understanding of the **Ground Size** attribute, we can see in the following screenshots how the shadows behave when the ground resolution isn't sufficient:

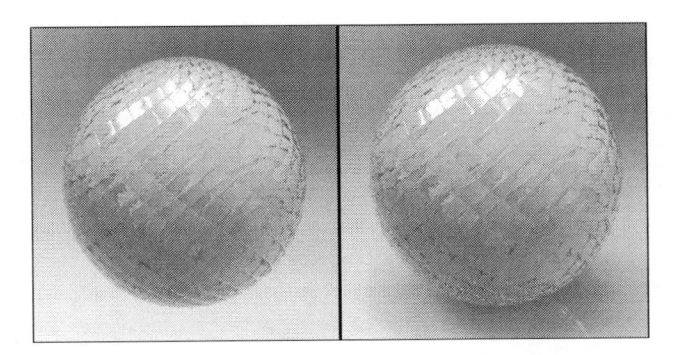

Lighting Made Easy

The screenshot on the left-hand side shows a sphere without any ground shadows and reflections, while the other one shows a sphere with ground shadows and reflections turned on.

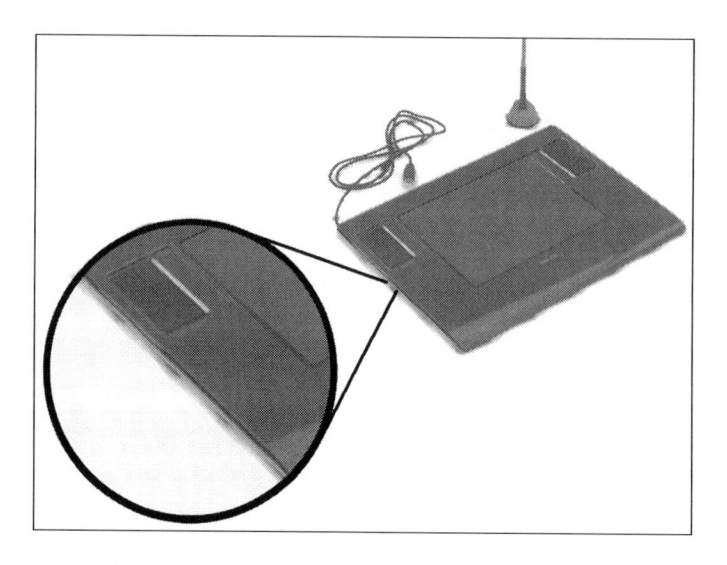

HDRI editor

The HDRI editor is a special feature only available in the Pro version of KeyShot. It lets us modify the look of our HDRIs in real time. The editor is located in the **Environment** tab next to the search bar.

Inside the editor there are two tabs, as follows:

- **Adjustments**: Here we will be able to see some of the parameters, such as **Saturation**, **Hue**, **Brightness**, and **Contrast**, that directly affect the HDRI that we have active in the scene. It is generally recommended to adjust with caution the properties in this tab, since doing so can give unrealistic results.

- **Pins**: This tab allows us to create light shapes that can be placed anywhere on our HDRIs to act as another light source or to simply add more intensity to certain areas of the image. We can change the shape of our light pin to be either circular or square, and we can also add other adjustments, such as **Radius**, **Color**, or **Falloff**.

We can see the editor in action, as shown in the following screenshot:

Since each project's needs are different, it is a good idea to experiment with each setting individually to develop a deeper understanding of the parameters. In our next discussion, we are going to take a look at the real-time settings, because they control other fundamental aspects of our lighting.

Real-time settings

In addition to the lighting properties found in the **Environment** tab, there is another set of parameters that can be found in the real-time settings section that provides further control over the lighting of our scene. However, these features are considered global properties, because the effects they produce affect the entire scene.

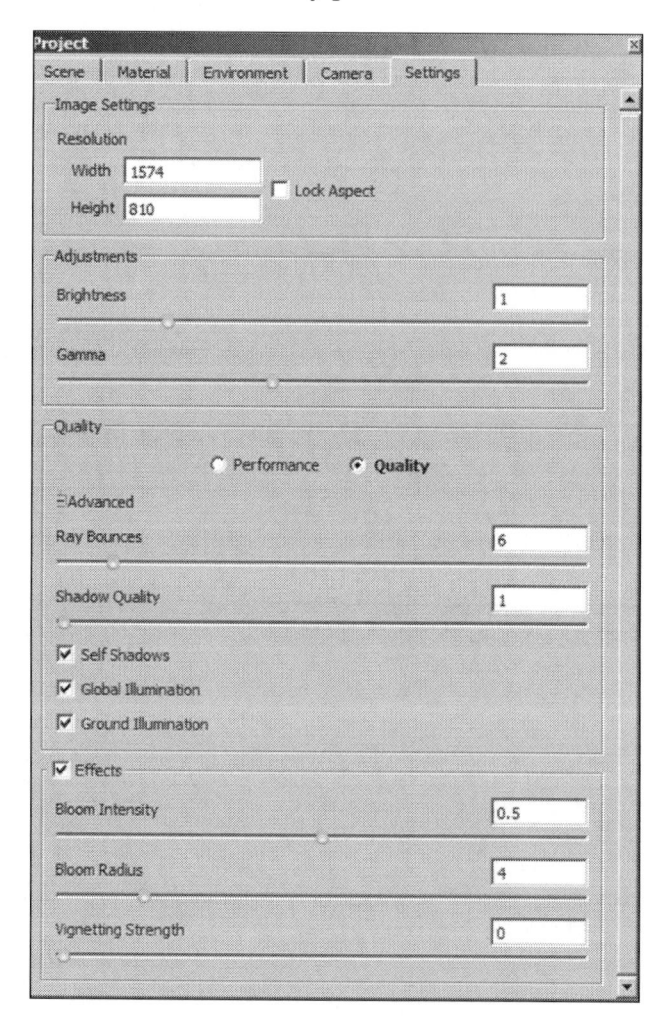

Parameters from the **Settings** tab affect the overall look of our scene. The following are some of the settings:

- **Lock Aspect**: Checking this checkbox from the **Settings** tab will lock our main viewport resolution to the values we have in the **Width** and **Height** fields respectively.

- **Brightness**: This parameter controls the brightness of the entire scene. According to KeyShot's online manual, this function is considered as a "post-process calculation applied to the real-time view", which means that any changes made in the brightness parameter will be shown in real time in our viewport and in the final rendered image.

- **Gamma**: This is another parameter that controls the brightness of an image. It is also considered a post-process calculation, meaning that any changes made to our **Gamma** parameter will be displayed in our viewport and also in the final rendered image.

  Briefly, gamma correction is a term used when an image is not rendered or displayed correctly onto our computer screens. Sometimes, our images may appear washed out or perhaps too dark after a rendering session. This is because the brightness and color channels of our images haven't been calibrated to be displayed properly on our monitors. By adjusting the **Gamma** slider, we can make corrections to the gamma of our scene and improve the overall intensity of the colors, contrast, and brightness.

- **Quality and Performance**: The **Quality** and **Performance** modes affect the real-time performance of KeyShot while the program is in use. If we select the **Performance** mode, KeyShot will not display certain features in real time to save computer resources, while if we select the **Quality** mode, effects such as **Ground Illumination** or **Ground Shadows** will be fully displayed in our viewport. By default, KeyShot is set to be displayed in the **Quality** mode.

- **Ray Bounces**: This refers to the number of times a ray of light can be bounced around the scene. The number of bounces can be significant if we are working with materials that are reflective or have refraction. When a ray of light hits a surface, whether it is reflected or refracted, it counts as a bounce, so increasing the value in our slider adds the number of times that a ray of light can travel within the scene until it dissipates. The effects can be seen in the following example; a sphere having a glass material applied to it:

In the preceding screenshot, the sphere on the left-hand side has **Ray Bounces** set to 1, while for the one on the right-hand side, **Ray Bounces** is set to 2.

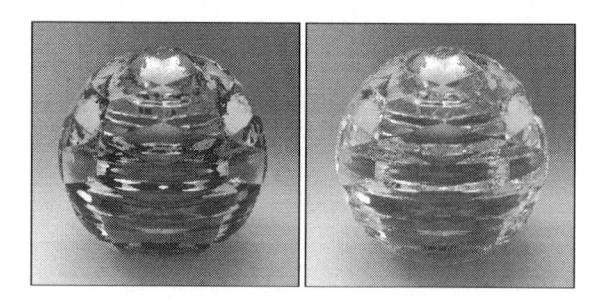

In the preceding screenshot, the sphere on the left-hand side has **Ray Bounces** set to 4, while for the one on the right-hand side, **Ray Bounces** is set to 12.

- **Shadow Quality**: This works in a similar way to **Ground Size**. Increasing the value on the slider will result in a more refined shadow, while decreasing the slider will make the shadows in the scene blockier. This parameter can be used independently of **Ground Size** and for this reason it consumes more resources. In fact, KeyShot recommends reducing the ground size first to increase the quality of our shadows, before using this parameter.

- **Self Shadows**: Checking this checkbox forces the object to project shadows on to itself. When it is used, it produces an effect similar to ambient occlusion. Shadows will be projected into areas of the object such as crevices and parts of the geometry that are in close proximity. We can toggle this effect by pressing the *S* key.

- **Global Illumination**: Checking this checkbox creates indirect lighting that when projected onto the geometry, will bounce off to another piece of the geometry, simulating a real environment. This parameter works in the same way as other global illumination properties found in various programs. We can toggle this effect by pressing the *I* key.

- **Bloom Intensity**: This produces an effect similar to a blur; it is also often used to enhance the glow on certain material properties such as highlights. It can also be used to produce softer edges or to increase the glow in emissive materials.

- **Vignetting Strength**: Increasing the slider creates a vignette effect.

The following are the screenshots showing showing one of our bullet scenes without any effects and another scene with bloom effect, respectively:

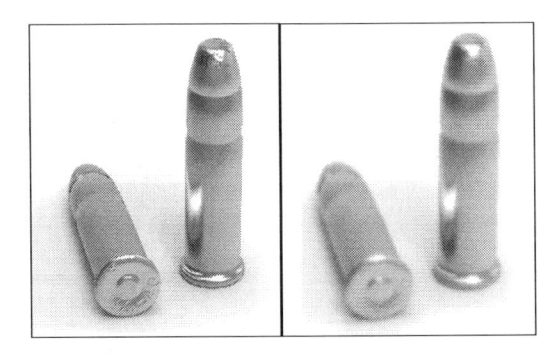

The following screenshot shows the bullet with a vignette effect:

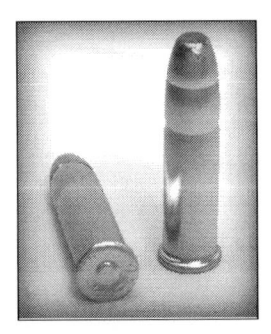

So far, we have covered a lot of ground by learning how to control the lighting in KeyShot, but there is also another group of settings that is equally important to understand. Since setting up the lighting for a scene many times depends on the configuration of our camera or view, I believe it is important to understand how to use and work with cameras for our projects.

Working with cameras

Setting up cameras for our projects inside KeyShot is a simple process. As always, when setting up a camera we need to understand what we are trying to achieve, whether it is a still shot or an animation. We will also discuss the camera attributes found in the **Camera** property tab.

To set up a camera for our project, let's continue where we left off with our tablet project. Perform the following steps:

1. Open up KeyShot.
2. Select **Open** from the **File** menu.
3. Let's find our project file, `Wacom_tablet`.

Lighting Made Easy

4. Click on **OK**.

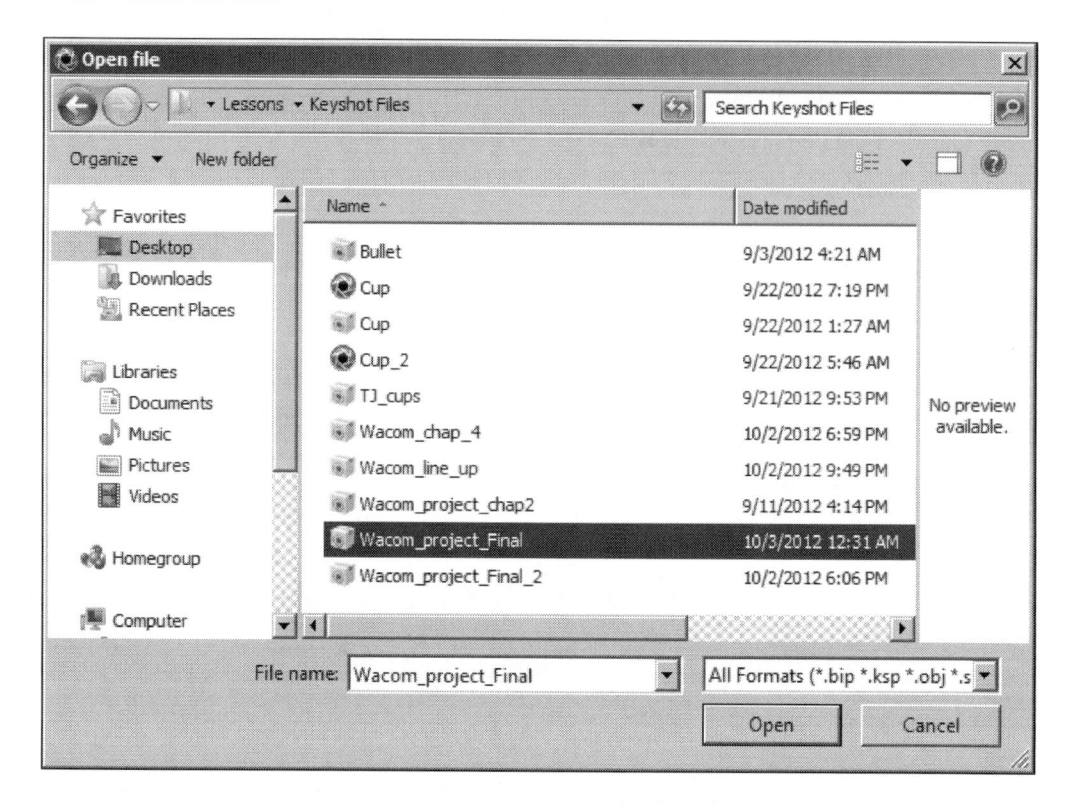

We can also find and load our project file from our disc, as we did previously at the beginning of this chapter. Perform the following steps to do so:

1. Open up KeyShot.
2. Select **Open** from the **File** menu.
3. Find `Wacom_project_Final.ksp` from our disc by navigating to **Lessons | Keyshot files**.
4. Click on **OK**.
5. From the new menu select the **Keep files in single folder** option.
6. This will open up the scene folder in KeyShot.
7. Right-click and select new folder and name it as `Wacom_final`.
8. Select the folder and click on **OK**.

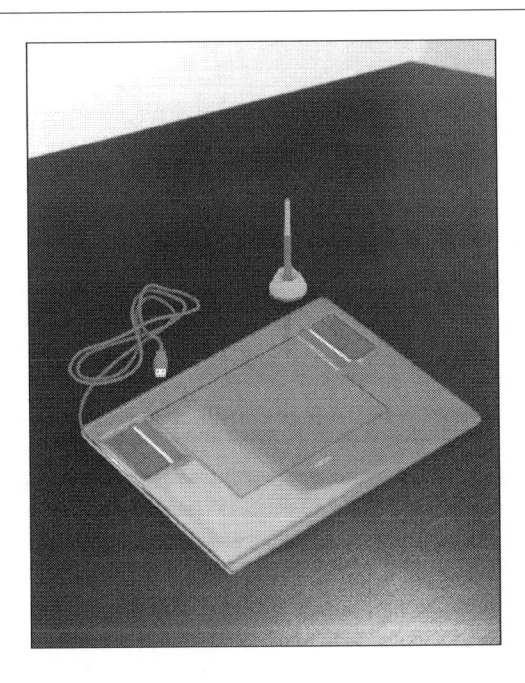

To understand how some of the settings work in the **Camera** tab, let's set our scene a little differently by changing our backplate, as follows:

1. Open up the **Library** window from our viewport.
2. Go to the **Backplates** tab.
3. Drag-and-drop **office_desk_24mm 2** to the scene.

Because we are using a new background, the orientation of our tablet is no longer correct. Let's move and rotate our tablet to place it onto the table. We might notice that the perspective of our tablet isn't correct compared to the perspective of our background. To remedy this issue perform the following steps:

1. After translating and rotating our object, and placing it on the desk, double-click anywhere on our tablet to open the **Project Editor** window.
2. Go to the **Camera** tab.
3. In the **Lens Setting** section, make sure that **Perspective** is selected instead of **Orthographic**.
4. Depending on the size of your monitor and resolution, you may have to adjust the zoom, perspective, scale of the object, and lighting differently. In our case, we are working with a 22-inch LG flat screen display with the resolution set to 1920 x 1080 pixels.

5. Decrease the **Perspective** slider to somewhere around to `18.845`.

   Other values for camera settings are as follows:
   - **Distance (Dolly)**: `12.792`
   - **Azimuth (Orbit)**: `42.086`
   - **Inclination (Elevation)**: `26.208`
   - **Twist**: `0`

6. Now that we have our tablet positioned at the angle we want, let's save our camera by clicking on the **+** symbol next to the camera list. Give the camera a name that is easy for you to remember.

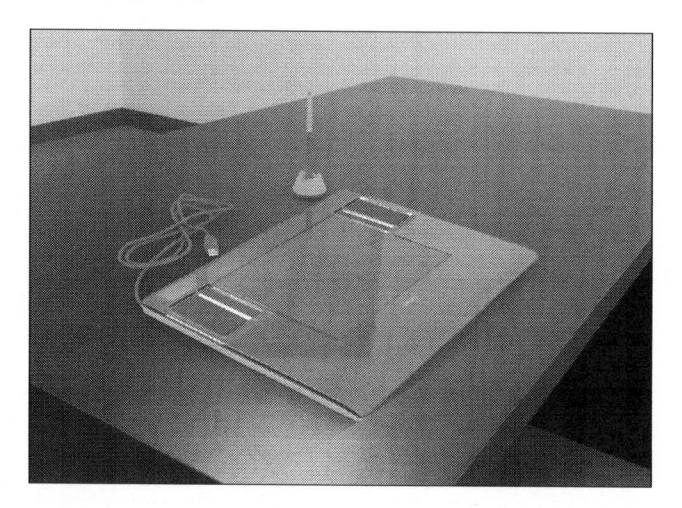

So far, our tablet is looking pretty good, but there are still some perspective and lighting issues that need to be corrected. Also, we can see that our tablet isn't completely resting on the desk. If we take a closer look at the shadows of our tablet and also the shadows under the pen holder, we can see that they are slightly off from the ground or in this case from the desk. Let's fix these issues, as follows:

1. Let's start by rotating our tablet slightly to the back by using the **Inclination** parameter.
2. Next let's move our tablet until it closely rests on our desk.
3. If you find it difficult to tell where the ground is in space, turn on the **Ground Grid** option from the **Settings** tab. This will help you with the placement of objects in space in relation to the ground. We can also use the snap to ground option by right-clicking on the object and selecting the **Move Object** option.

4. Once we have finished applying changes to our tablet, let's go ahead and lock our camera by clicking on **Unlocked** next to the camera list.
5. Now our camera should be locked, and all sliders and parameters should be grayed out to avoid any accidental changes.
6. Since the scene has been modified, we need to adjust the lighting as well.
7. Let's go to the **Environment** tab and input the following values:
    - **Contrast**: 0.34
    - **Brightness**: 2.04
    - **Size**: 44.71
    - **Height**: 0.011
    - **Rotation**: 245
    - **Ground Size**: 6.235

Now we can see that our tablet has more accurate reflections and the perspective has improved. I believe the lighting can be a little stronger. So far, we have covered the basics of how to manipulate our camera; let's take a look at the attributes in the **Camera** tab next.

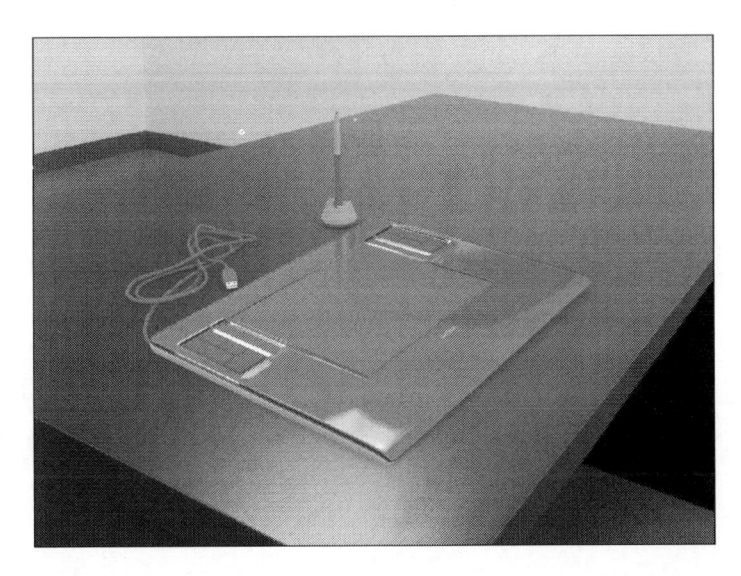

In the preceding screenshot the brightness has been toned down to match the soft lighting in the backplate.

Camera attributes

The following is the list of attributes in the **Camera** tab:

- **Camera list**: By clicking on the arrow, we will be shown a drop-down list with all the cameras available in the scene. By selecting one of the cameras, it becomes active in our viewport, but keep in mind that cameras will become unlocked once we select them.

- **Creating and deleting cameras**: To create a new camera, click on the + symbol and KeyShot will automatically create a new camera based on viewport. Clicking on the - (minus) symbol deletes the camera that is currently active from the camera list.

- **Locking cameras**: We can lock the view of our cameras by clicking on the **Unlocked** button on the left-hand side of the camera list. Once a camera is locked, all its attributes will be locked as well. The **Edit Mode** button unlocks the camera that is currently active. Also, by switching from one camera to another that was previously locked, the active camera becomes unlocked.

- **Distance (Dolly)**: This allows us to move the camera closer to or further away from our object. The distance is calculated from the center of the scene. We can also control the distance by pressing the *Alt* key and right-clicking and dragging left or right.

- **Azimuth (Orbit)**: We can use this slider to rotate around the y axis of our object. To determine the location of the axis that the camera will rotate about, we will use the **"look at" point** option. Clicking the **"look at" point** button and clicking anywhere in our object will let us place a point of origin for the camera to rotate.

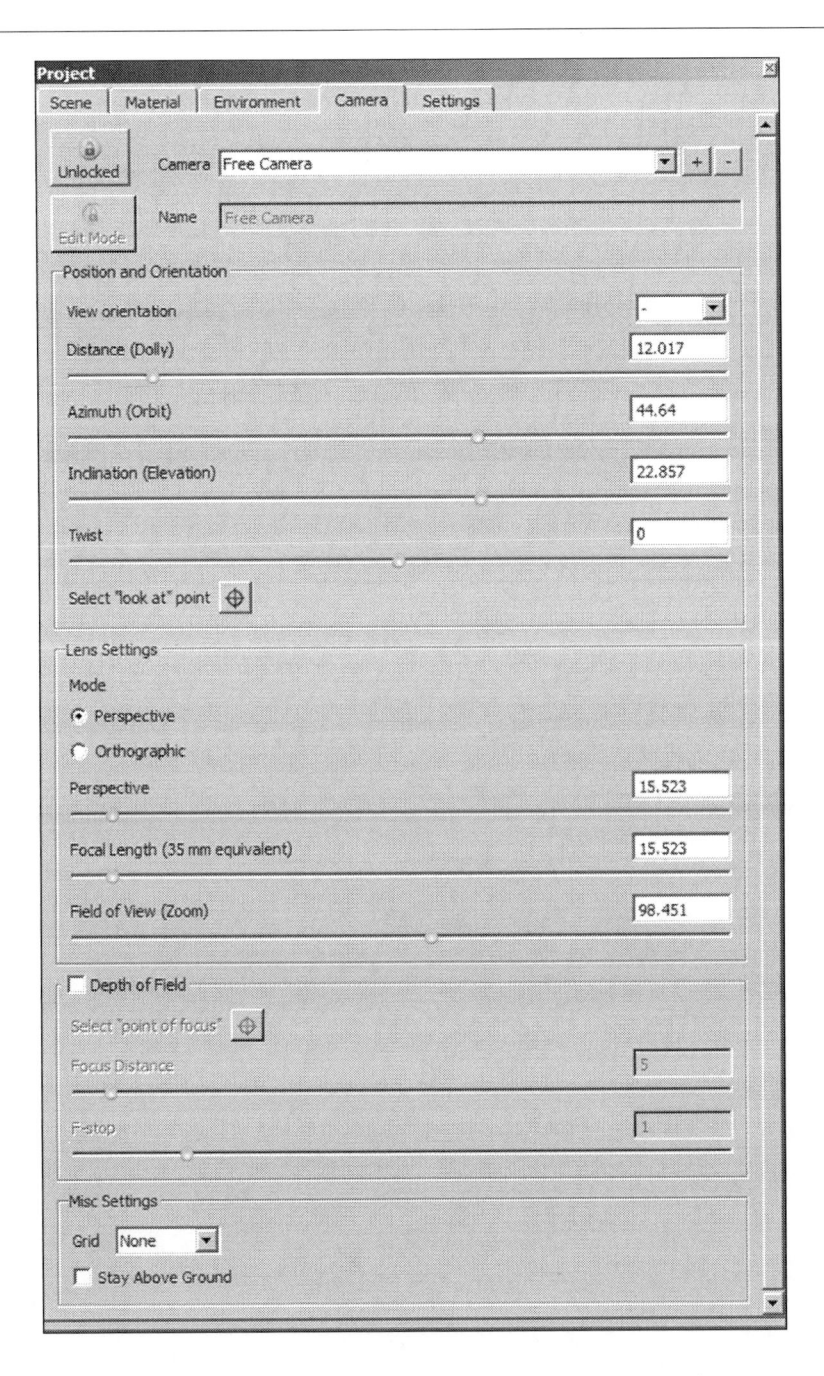

- **Inclination (Elevation)**: This attribute allows us to rotate the camera about the x axis to see either the top or the bottom of an object. It is also dependent on the **"look at" point** option.

- **Twist**: This works similarly to **Inclination** or **Azimuth**, but it allows us to rotate the camera around the z axis.
- **"look at" point**: This is a button displayed with a target symbol. When this tool is activated, it changes the appearance of our mouse cursor from an arrow into a target symbol. When we click on a part of our object, the **"look at" point** option will make that area appear at the center of focus. This attribute also sets the point of origin for other parameters such as **Azimuth** or **Distance** to work properly. It is also often used to create a center rotation for a camera, which allows us to make turntable animations.
- **Perspective**: This is one of the two modes that we can choose for our cameras found in the **Lens Settings** section. Once we turn on this option for our camera, our **Perspective** slider becomes available, which will allow us to show objects becoming smaller and conveying together in the horizon as they appear further away from our camera.
- **Orthographic**: This is the second projection mode found in our **Lens Settings** section. When orthographic projection is used, it will gray out the **Perspective** slider and will ignore any perspective effects as well. It will basically try to make our 3D object appear in a 2D representation.
- **Focal Length**: This attribute works as multiple lenses in a real camera. Increasing the value on the **Focal Length** slider will make our camera zoom into our object producing the same effect of a real lens. We should not confuse this with the **Distance (Dolly)** effect, since the camera position remains the same. Reducing the value of **Focal Length** produces a wider angle view. The following screenshot shows a view from a camera with the **Perspective** mode:

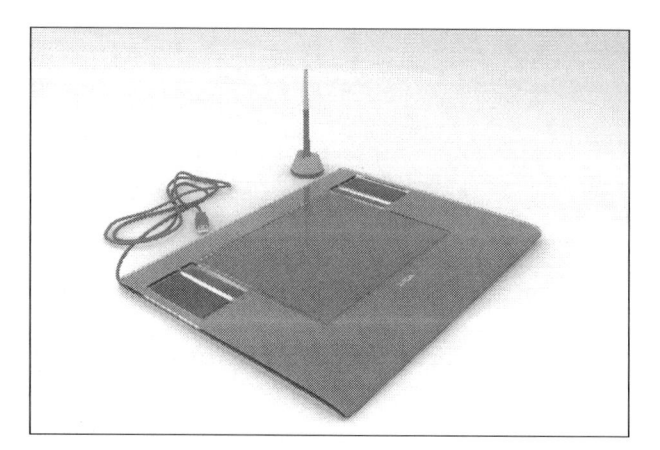

The following screenshot shows a view from a camera with the **Orthographic** mode:

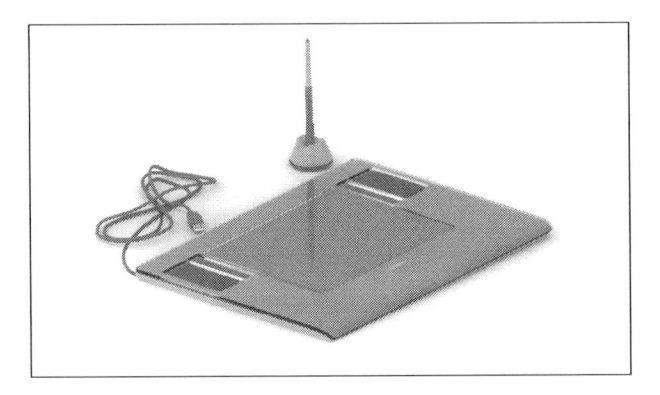

- **Depth of Field**: This option lets us create areas of attention by blurring other areas of an image. In order to use **Depth of Field**, we need to know which part of the scene we want to place our focus on. For this we use the **"point of focus"** option which works in a similar way to the **"look at" point** option.
- **"point of focus"**: This creates an area of attention in an image when using **Depth of Field**. The area of focus can be used to either create an area of focus by blurring the rest of the image or vice versa. Blur can also be applied to the area of focus, by using the **Focus Distance** option, to keep the rest of the image sharp.
- **Focus Distance**: This can be understood as the distance in which the blur or sharpness takes place from the focal point. By increasing the value on the **Focus Distance** slider, the focus area shifts farther away from its original position, which makes other parts of the image come in focus.
- **F-stop**: This works the same way as the f-numbers of a real camera. It represents the lens speed and it controls the amount of blurriness. Setting **F-stop** to lower values increases blurriness in the image, while higher values lessen the effect. However, the **Depth of Field** effect is dependent on both **Focus Distance** and **F-stop**.

The following example shows two screenshots with their focus point placed on the bullet closest to the camera, but both have different focal distances and F-stops. The screenshot on the left-hand side shows a bullet with low focal distance and less F-stops, while the one on the right-hand side shows a bullet with high focal distance and moderate F-stops:

We have covered up to this point all the core subjects and fundamentals of using KeyShot to render out our projects. Understanding how materials, lighting, and cameras can be set up, KeyShot can speed up our workflow while working with more complex models. It is always good practice to keep in mind that KeyShot is not a modeling program; it is only a rendering application, so it is recommended that at the end of any project, if our plan is to use KeyShot, we should prepare our models accordingly.

Let's go ahead now and start a new project and practice applying some of the materials we have covered.

Insulated cup

For the next project, we are going to texture and render an insulated cup. Let's start by opening up KeyShot, and perform the following steps:

1. Select **Import** from our viewport.
2. Next find and import the `Cup.obj` file. It is located at **Lessons | Keyshot models | data**.
3. Click on **OK**.

Let's start applying a material to our cup. Perform the following steps:

1. Click on the **Library** icon and open the **Library** window from the viewport.
2. Go to the **Materials** tab.
3. Let's find the material, **Clear shiny plastic – red** by navigating to
4. **Plastic | Clear | Shiny | Basic**.
5. Drag-and-drop the material onto our cup.

Since most cups have patterns or indentures, let's add a bump map to make our cup look more interesting. Perform the following steps:

1. Double-click anywhere on our cup to open the **Project Editor** window.
2. Go to the **Material** tab.
3. Inside the **Material** tab, go to the **Texture** tab and activate the bump channel.
4. Once a new window opens, scroll down to find **tile_bump.jpg**.
5. Click on **OK**.
6. Once the map is loaded, change the mapping method to **Cylindrical**.
7. Let's set **Scale** to `1.065` and **Bump Height** to `0.67`.
8. Since it is a bump map, scroll down in the **Texture** menu and uncheck the **Normal Map** option.
9. Make sure the **Repeat** checkbox is checked.

Lighting Made Easy

10. Go to the **Environment** tab and set **Ground Size** to `6.235`.

Next, let's apply a material for the rubber pad of our cup. Perform the following steps to do so:

1. Open the **Library** window again and type in `Rubber` in the search bar located in the upper-right corner of the **Materials** tab.
2. Drag-and-drop this material to the heat isolation pad of our cup.
3. Double-click anywhere on the cup to open the **Project Editor** window.
4. Change the diffuse color from the **Properties** tab to a yellowish or a cream color. Change the values of the following parameters:
    - **Hue**: `39`
    - **Saturation**: `193`
    - **Value**: `170`
    - **Red**: `170`
    - **Green**: `125`
    - **Blue**: `41`

   I opted for the colors as shown in the following screenshot:

[76]

For our straw, let's apply a cooler color to counter our red cup. Perform the following steps to do so:

1. For our straw I selected **Shiny cloudy plastic – deep tur**, which can be found by navigating to **Plastic | Cloudy | Shiny | Serene**.
2. Drag-and-drop it on our straw.
3. As I thought the color was a little too bright, I slightly reduced the **Specular Transmission** value.

This produces the following screenshot:

Lighting Made Easy

Lastly, for our lid, let's apply a transparent colorless plastic. Perform the following steps to do so:

1. The material used is **Clear white shiny**, which can be found at **Plastic | Clear | Shiny | Basic**.
2. Again drag-and-drop the material onto our lid.
3. Change the value of our **Diffuse** channel to make it appear more cloudy.
4. Optionally, we can also add a bump map to our lid, as follows:
    1. Double-click on the lid to open the **Project Editor** window.
    2. Go to **Material | Texture**.
    3. Activate the bump channel.
    4. We can choose a file such as `mesh_circular_normal.jpg` or similar.

This changes the lid of our cup, as can be seen in the following screenshot:

We have finished applying materials to our cup. As we can see, it looks pretty good with the standard materials and textures from KeyShot. However, so far we haven't modified the lighting.

Let's proceed now with changing the lighting. Perform the following steps to do so:

1. Open up the **Library** window.
2. Go to the **Environments** tab.
3. Find the overhead array, **2k.hdr**, by navigating to **Studio | Panel | Overhead**.

4. Input the following values:
    - **Contrast**: 1
    - **Brightness**: 1.725
    - **Size**: 27.04
    - **Height**: -0.288
    - **Rotation**: 358
5. For our background, let's choose a solid color. Make the background color somewhat red or pinkish.
6. Check the checkboxes for **Ground Shadows** and **Ground Reflections**.
7. Set **Ground Size** to 6.235.

After finishing with modifying the attributes from the **Environment** tab, let's go to the **Settings** tab and make additional changes to our lighting, as follows:

1. Set **Brightness** to 1.105.
2. Also set **Gamma** to 1.75.
3. Leave **Ray Bounces** at 6.
4. Let's make sure now that all the following checkboxes are checked:
    - **Self Shadow**
    - **Global Illumination**
    - **Ground Illumination**
5. We are also going to add the vignette and bloom effects to our cup.
6. Check on the **Effects** tab.
7. Input the following values:
    - **Bloom Intensity**: 0.672
    - **Bloom Radius**: 10.576
    - **Vignette Strength**: 0.702

This would produce the following screenshot:

8. Lastly, let's create a camera facing the cup by its side and save it.
9. Select the **Render** icon from the main viewport.
10. For now let's just change the properties in the **Output** category.
11. Once we have chosen a name, resolution, and format, click on **Render**.

KeyShot will take a few minutes to render the image, depending on the specification of your computer, and it will save the final image in the `Rendering` folder of KeyShot's `resource` folder found on the desktop.

Duplicating models

From this point we can create more cups, where each one will be slightly different from the others, with its own color and patterns. This way we can quickly set up a product catalog if we wish or a product presentation lineup.

Let's continue working on our project:

1. Go to the **Camera** tab.
2. From the camera list select **Free Camera**.
3. Go to the **Scene** tab and select the **Cup** node to have the entire model selected.
4. Right-click on the **Cup** node and select the **Duplicate** option.

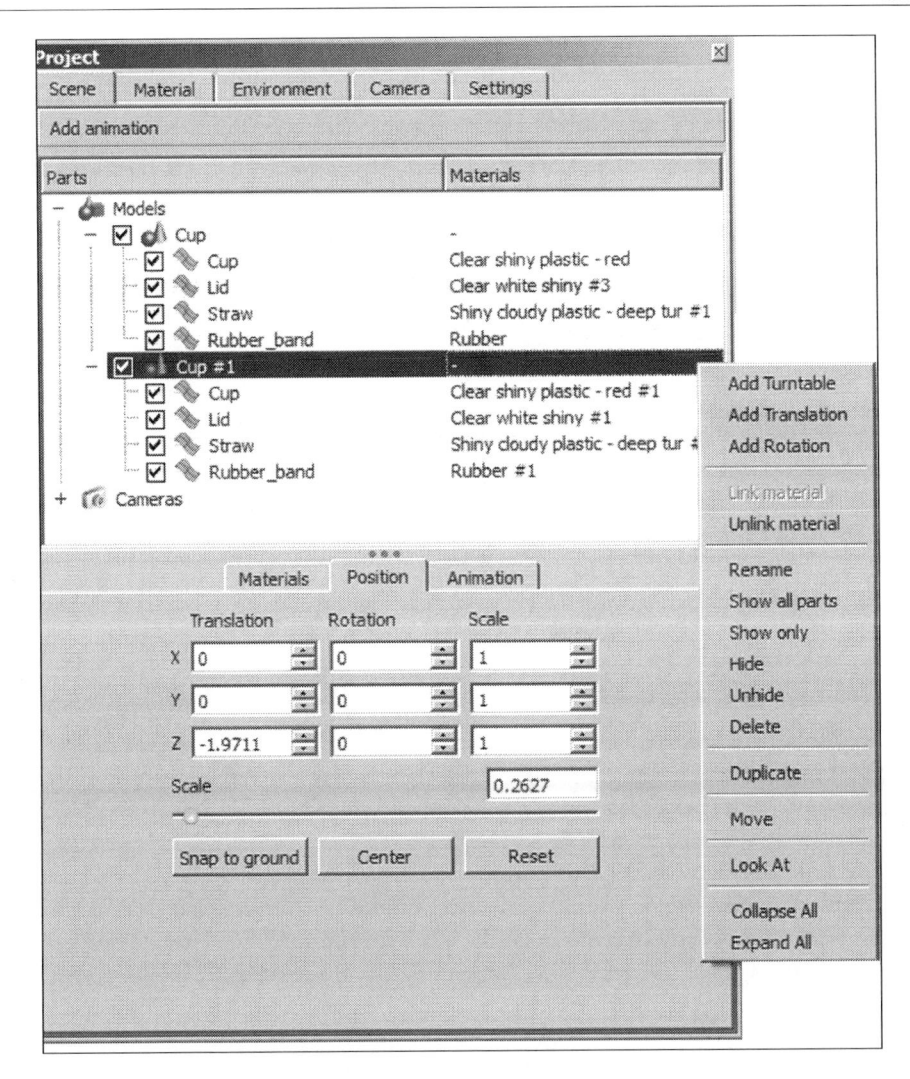

![Project dialog screenshot showing Parts tree with Cup and Cup #1 expanded, and a right-click context menu with options including Add Turntable, Add Translation, Add Rotation, Link material, Unlink material, Rename, Show all parts, Show only, Hide, Unhide, Delete, Duplicate, Move, Look At, Collapse All, Expand All.]

This will create a duplicate copy of our original cup with its own set of materials and textures.

5. The newly created cup should be renamed as **Cup #1**.

Lighting Made Easy

6. With **Cup #1** highlighted, move the entire model so that it sits right next to our original cup, as shown in the following example:

We have now learned how to duplicate an object and still preserve all its original textures and materials. This can be done for individuals parts as well.

Duplicating objects can be very useful sometimes, since we can use the duplicate as a reference to run tests with materials and textures. Now let's repeat the process and duplicate our cup, until we have around six or seven of them lined up with each other.

Since our final objective is to create a lineup of the same product, all we have to do now is to change the colors of our cups and straws to give our final image a little bit more variety. We can also experiment with the bloom intensity and vignette effects to create different looks. There are always other ways to present our work; one of them can be arranging our cups in a specific way, or using our camera and experimenting with the perspective.

In the following example, we decided to change the color of our background to a light blue or purple. We have also added ground reflections and global illumination. Ray bounces were set a bit higher to add to our cups a little bit more detail. Also, we can see that **Depth of Field** has been added to the camera:

Alternatively, the following is also another way to present our work:

Always try to experiment with new ways of presenting your projects. Clients love to see variety and versatility when viewing a product presentation.

Summary

In this chapter we saw that KeyShot can completely depend on HDRIs for lighting. Before adjusting the lighting, first we need to think how our projects will look in the end. Since Keyshot is primarily dependent on HDRIs, we recommend to use the high-quality images. The Environment tab, located inside the Project Editor window, contains all the parameters that control the lighting of our scene. Among these properties we have Contrast, Brightness, Size, Height, and Rotation.

Lighting Made Easy

A new feature called the HDRI Editor allows us to directly manipulate our HDRIs and to make changes such as the hue or contrast of the images. We can also add lighting spots, which are called pins, to anywhere in the image and they serve as another source of lighting. The HDRI Editor is available by purchasing the professional version of KeyShot 3.

We also learned that real-time settings can also contribute to the lighting in our scene. There are two parameters that can be easily confused since both control the brightness of our scene. The first parameter is Brightness, which controls the amount of brightness intensity overall in the scene and the second one is Gamma, which controls the amount of compensation needed of brightness and contrast of our scene to be displayed correctly on our monitors. It is recommended to leave the Gamma value at default in the real-time settings tab.

Other important attributes we discussed are Global Illumination and Shadow quality, which are used in almost in every project of KeyShot because they help help to simulate real environment lighting.

We can create a new camera by clicking the plus (+) icon located in the camera tab inside the project editor. To delete a camera simply select the camera we want to erase and click on the - (subtract) button.

We have also studied the function of each camera attribute. To create the Depth of Field effect, make sure that the checkbox of the feature has been checked, and increase or decrease the values of the Focus Distance and F-stops sliders.

Lastly, we mentioned how to duplicate objects in our scene by going to the Scene tab and right click on the object or model we want to duplicate. Select duplicate and move the newly duplicated object aside in the scene.

In the next chapter, we are going to learn how to render in KeyShot. We are also going to examine how to create a turntable animation.

4
Showcasing and Product Presentation

In the last chapter we covered the basics of rendering in KeyShot. In order to take our projects to the next level and wrap our designs for a product presentation, we will take a look at the different ways in which we can showcase our product. We will also need to understand what the rendering settings and options can do for us. This will help us save time, and allow us to find methods and ways to achieve greater quality in our final renders.

In this chapter you will learn:

- Setting our Wacom project for a lineup
- Render properties and options
- Creating our own turntable cycle for product presentation

Preparing our project

Before we render out any scene, whether an animation or just a still image, we need to make sure our projects are properly set up. This means that the better understanding we have regarding the lighting conditions, materials, shadows, and real-time parameters, the easier it will be to set up our render according to our needs. For this chapter, we will work with our Wacom tablet project again, but this time we are going to create a lineup presentation. We are also going to create a turntable animation using our **Cup** project.

Let's get started with our Wacom project. Perform the following steps:

1. Open up KeyShot.
2. Select **Open**.

3. Load up our **Wacom_tablet** project from where we left off in *Chapter 2, Understanding Materials and Textures*.
4. Alternatively, we can open our project from our disc, as we did in the previous projects.
5. Find **Wacom_project_Final.ksp** from our disc by navigating to **Lessons | Keyshot files**.
6. Click on **OK**.
7. From the new menu select the **Keep files in one folder** option.
8. This will open up the scene folder in KeyShot.
9. Right-click and select new folder and name it as Wacom_final.
10. Select the folder and click on **OK**.

Once our project loads up, let's erase the entire USB cable as well as the pen and the pen holder cup by performing the following steps:

1. Open the **Library** window.
2. Go to the **Scene** tab.
3. Select the parts for the pen, USB cable, and pen holder.
4. Once selected go to our viewport, right-click and select **Delete parts from the menu**.
5. Click on **Accept**.

Next, let's rotate our tablet and move our camera upwards so that we can look at our tablet straight from the top, as shown in the following example:

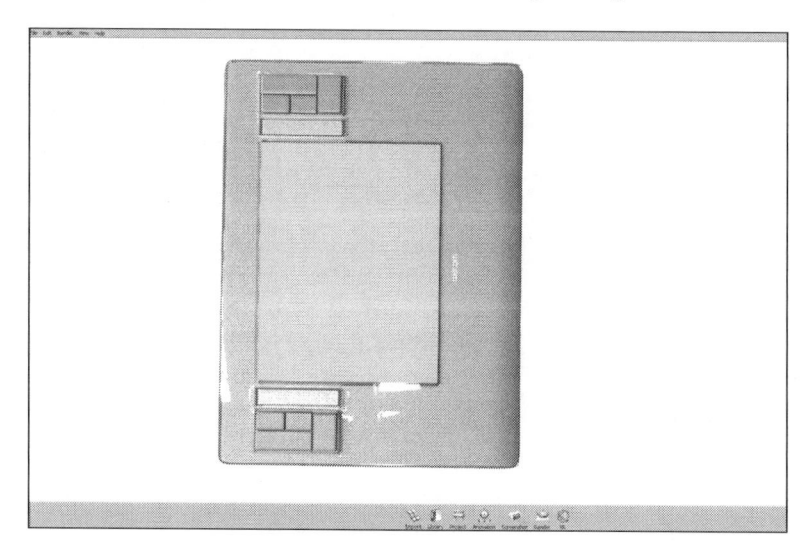

Since we are changing our angle of view, we will need to modify the lighting as well, to get a better positioning of our highlights and shadows. In this case we are using the `hdri-locations_factory_4k` environment file, since it is a well-balanced HDRI for our purposes. Next, I have listed the parameters from my **Environment** tab along with their values:

- **Contrast**: `1.002`
- **Brightness**: `1.415`
- **Size**: `92.02`
- **Height**: `0.5`
- **Rotation**: `218`

Note that these values will vary depending on how our camera has been placed. As we mentioned before, we should have the camera positioning set before making changes to our lighting. Any parameters such as the distance of the camera or the rotation will affect the placement of our lighting.

After the placement is set, let's add the new camera and save our current position in it. Perform the following steps:

1. Open the **Project Editor** window by double-clicking on our tablet.
2. Go to the **Camera** tab.
3. Click on the **+** (add) symbol to add a new camera.
4. Freeze the camera by clicking on the locker button on the left-hand side of the camera list.

To create a lineup presentation for this project, we need to first duplicate our model to create multiple versions of it and to have each one assigned with a different color, similar to our cup example from the previous chapter.

To start the duplicate process perform the following steps:

1. Open the **Library** window and go the **Scene** tab.
2. Select our Wacom model in its entirety.
3. Right-click and select **Duplicate**; this will create a duplicate copy of our tablet.
4. Select the second tablet from the scene tree.
5. With the second tablet selected, go to our viewport and right-click.

6. Then select the **Move Object** option to move the tablet slightly to the right.

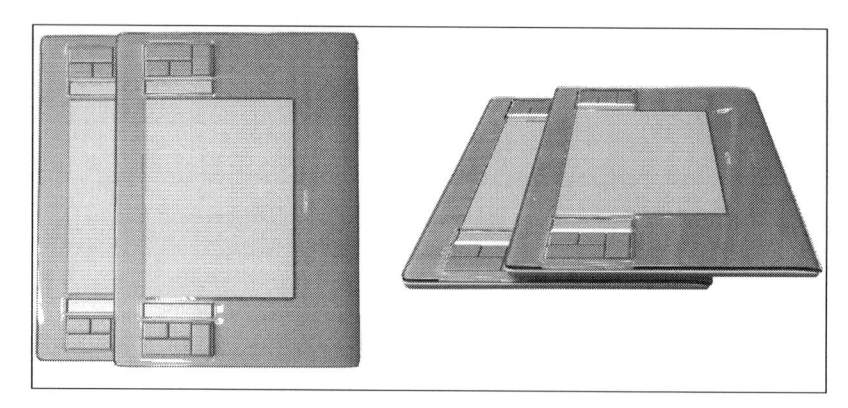

Now, to start assigning a different color to our second tablet, we need to perform the following steps:

1. Hide the transparent cover that sits on top of our tablet by right-clicking on the cover and selecting the **Hide Part** option.
2. Then double-click on the surface of the tablet.
3. Once the **Project Editor** window is open, go to the **Material** tab.
4. In the **Diffuse** attribute change the color to one of your preferences.

Repeat the same process for the other variations of the tablet, as shown in the following example:

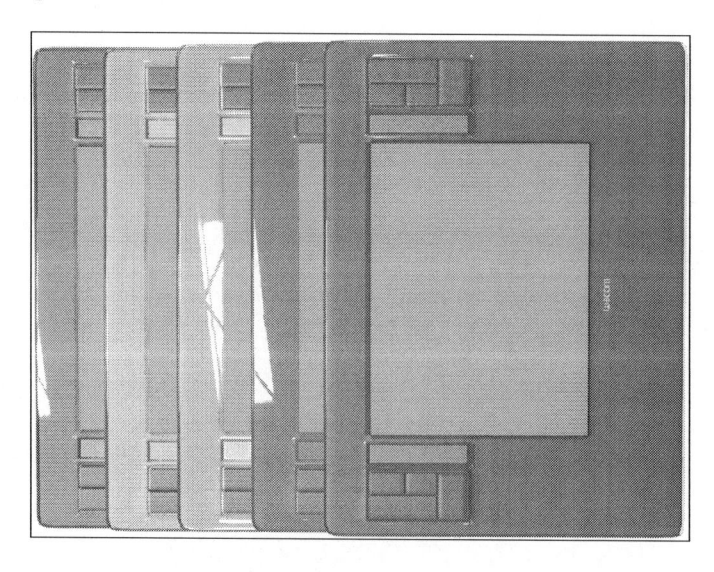

Creating different iterations of our model helps us provide visual interest when the time comes to submit a product presentation. In this example, we wanted to demonstrate the ease with which KeyShot can tackle this task by simply changing the color of our original product without making major changes to the scene. Having multiple models can also help us detect problems with lighting, the look of the material, or problems with the model itself.

Since we have most of our scene ready, we can now take a look at the parameters in the **Render** tab to better understand their functions.

Rendering in KeyShot

After our scene gets set up, the rendering process is the last stage of our workflow inside KeyShot. It is important to understand how the **Render** window's properties work, since changing the values of the attributes found in this menu to high or low values can impact the results of our renders significantly.

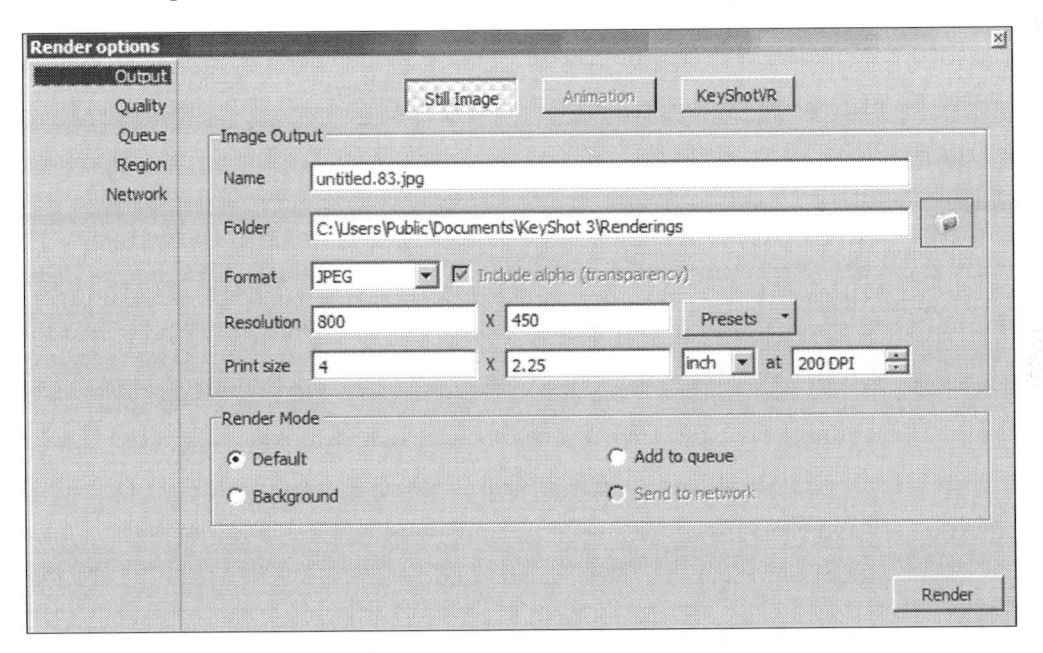

To open the **Render** menu, press the **Render** (teapot) icon from the viewport and the **Render options** window will open with five submenus, as shown in the preceding screenshot. Those submenus are described in the following sections.

Output menu

The **Output** menu controls the overall final settings of the image file that will undergo the rendering process. Some of the features are as follows:

- **Format**: This lets us choose the type of file we want to output. Currently KeyShot can output the formats such as EXR, JPEG, PNG, TIFF, and TIFF 32 Bit.
- **Resolution**: This allows us to input the final resolution of our image. It also provides predetermined image sizes that are commonly used.
- **Print size**: This controls the actual size of the image and not the resolution size.
- **Render Mode**: The **Default** mode lets us see the rendering process while the image is being output. If we change **Render Mode** to **Add to queue**, we will assign a rendering task that will be added to the list found in the **Queue** submenu. Lastly, if we chose the **Background** mode, KeyShot will not show the render progress of our model, but instead the process will take place in memory. By changing our **Render Mode** to **Background**, we can save resources and increase the computer's performance.

Quality menu

The following are some of the features of the **Quality** menu:

- **Samples**: This controls the amount of information that will be rendered at the pixel level. Higher values will increase the accuracy of the pixel information, which produces images of higher quality in return. However, increasing the amount of sampling will also increase the render time. KeyShot's online manual suggests leaving this as a global setting between the values of 8 to 16 and controlling the local sampling from the material's settings.
- **Global illumination quality**: This slider controls the overall accuracy of all the indirect lighting in the scene.
- **Ray bounces**: This lets us choose how many times we want to let the rays in our scene to hit and bounce between surfaces, objects, and the overall environment. This slider works the same as the **Ray Bounces** attribute found in the real-time settings, but at a global scale.
- **Pixel filter size**: By increasing the value of this slider, it creates a blurry or soft look in our images without increasing render time.
- **Anti aliasing**: Increasing the value of this slider will render our images with softer and smoother edges, but it will also increase the render time.

- **DOF quality**: This is another global attribute that controls the smoothness or the graininess effect in an image with DOF applied. Raising the value of **DOF quality** will increase the smoothness effect, but it will also increase render time.

- **Shadow quality**: This controls the quality of our ground shadows in the scene. KeyShot's online manual suggests to work with the attributes of the real-time settings before determining what values should be used for the Sharp Shadows slider.

- **Sharp shadows**: This checkbox allows objects in the scene to cast sharp shadows on each other. It is checked by default and KeyShot suggests leaving it checked for increased accuracy.

- **Sharper texture filtering**: This checkbox forces KeyShot to try to maintain the quality of the textures when certain areas of a geometry compress the texture. It is recommended by KeyShot to also leave this checkbox, checked for increased accuracy.

Queue menu

We can use this menu whenever we want to add render tasks to the queue list. Tasks can be added or removed from the list using the **Add job** or **Delete job** button, respectively.

When a task or a job is added to the list, rendering will occur with the settings and values placed on the scene, at the moment when the task is added to the queue. Tasks at the top get higher priority at render time. To move a task up or down for changing priority, just select the task and click on the **Move up** or **Move down** button, as shown in the following screenshot:

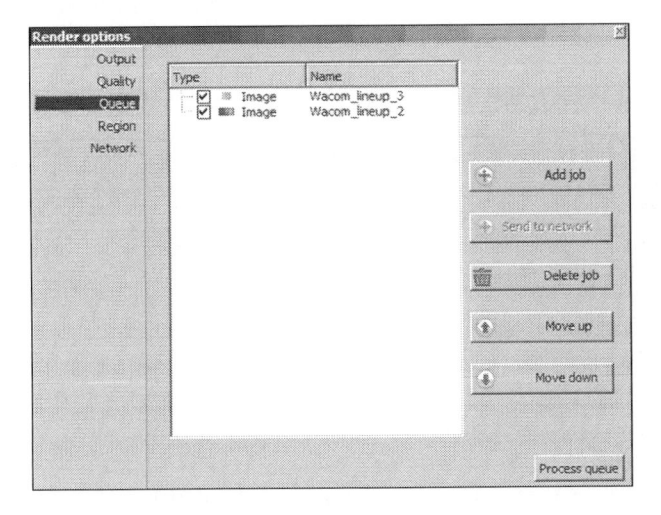

Region menu

Region Render is a powerful feature that allows us to render only a portion of the scene, which lets us save time and make quick changes to our project. **Region Render** is a feature available only in KeyShot Pro and other premium versions of the package. To use the **Region Render** option just simply go over the **Region** submenu and enable the feature. In the menu, there will be also a menu that allows us to set the width and height of the render box.

Network menu

KeyShot also features a network rendering system, known as a render farm in other applications. Render jobs can be added to the network rendering system and can have multiple computers processing the same task. This feature, however, needs to be installed on multiple computers, and it consists of three main elements in order to create a network, as follows:

- **Master**: The master unit is where the jobs and assignments are submitted from the client units, and then distributed to the slave units for the rendering to take place. According to KeyShot's online manual, master units also hold the licenses that specify how many CPU cores are allowed in the network system.
- **Client**: This serves as the unit where the jobs are scheduled and then submitted to the master unit.
- **Slave**: These units are in charge of processing all the jobs submitted. The rendering calculations occur at the slave units and are then sent back to the master unit.

Now that we have studied and reviewed some of the settings in the **Render options** window, we can take this knowledge and apply it to our future projects. It is important to remember that most of the settings in the **Render** menu affect the scene globally; so when making modifications to the settings in this menu, always start with low values and gradually increase the values to obtain the desired effect.

For testing purposes, let's have a look at the following example:

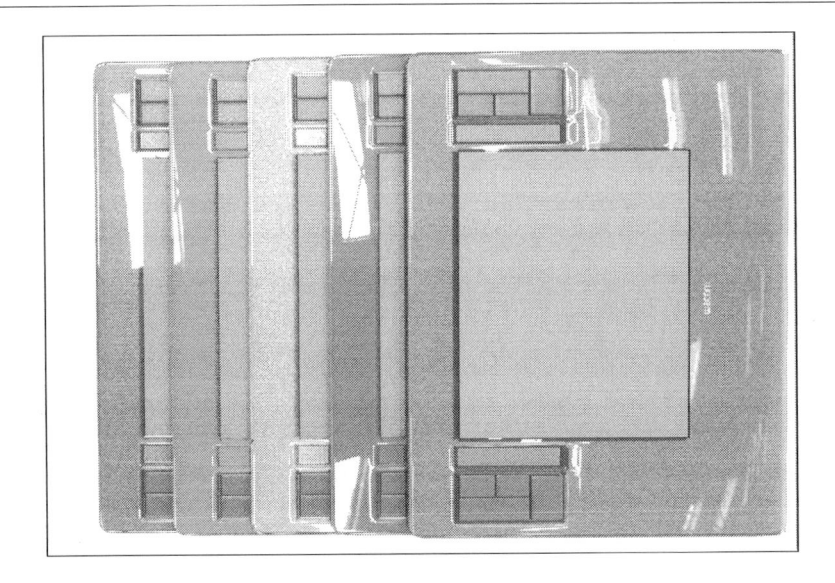

I decided to change the surface material of all the tablets in our lineup from our original plastic material to a new metallic car paint material. This new material offers two interesting new features, **Metal Flake Size** and **Metal Flake Visibility**. By modifying the two values, we can add small metal flakes into our material, similar to what we see in car paint. Then, for our final render, we increased the sampling and the ray bounces to give a more polished look.

Creating a turntable presentation

To create our turntable presentation we are going to use our cup model from the previous chapter. Perform the following steps:

1. Open up KeyShot.
2. Select **Open** and load up our Cup file.
3. Once Cup is loaded, hide our other two cups leaving only the red one in the scene.

4. Next, click on the **Animation** icon from our viewport to open the **Animation** window, as shown in the following screenshot:

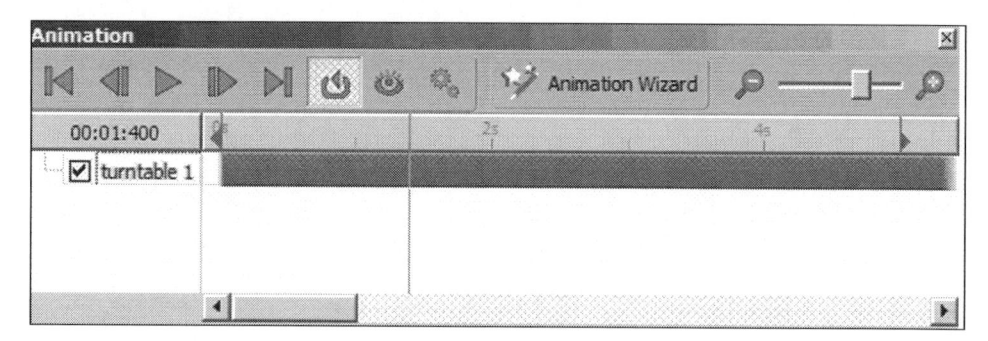

5. Click on the **Animation Wizard** icon.
6. A new window should appear with different types of animation at our disposal.
7. For our exercise, let's select the turntable animation and click on **OK**.
8. Now we are going to select an object or a model that will have the turntable animation.
9. In this case we will select the red cup and click on **OK**.
10. Once in the **Settings** window, you can add your own preferences, such as how long you want the turntable animation to last for. It also gives us options such as **Ease in** and **Ease out** for our animation.
11. Click on **OK** or **Next** once we are done with the preferences.

Notice now that a new animation sequence has been added to our animation timeline. We can go ahead and play the animation to see how it looks. At any time we can erase or edit our animation by clicking and highlighting our animation sequence and then going to the **Scene** tab in our **Project** window. The animation settings will again become available to us for making changes if necessary.

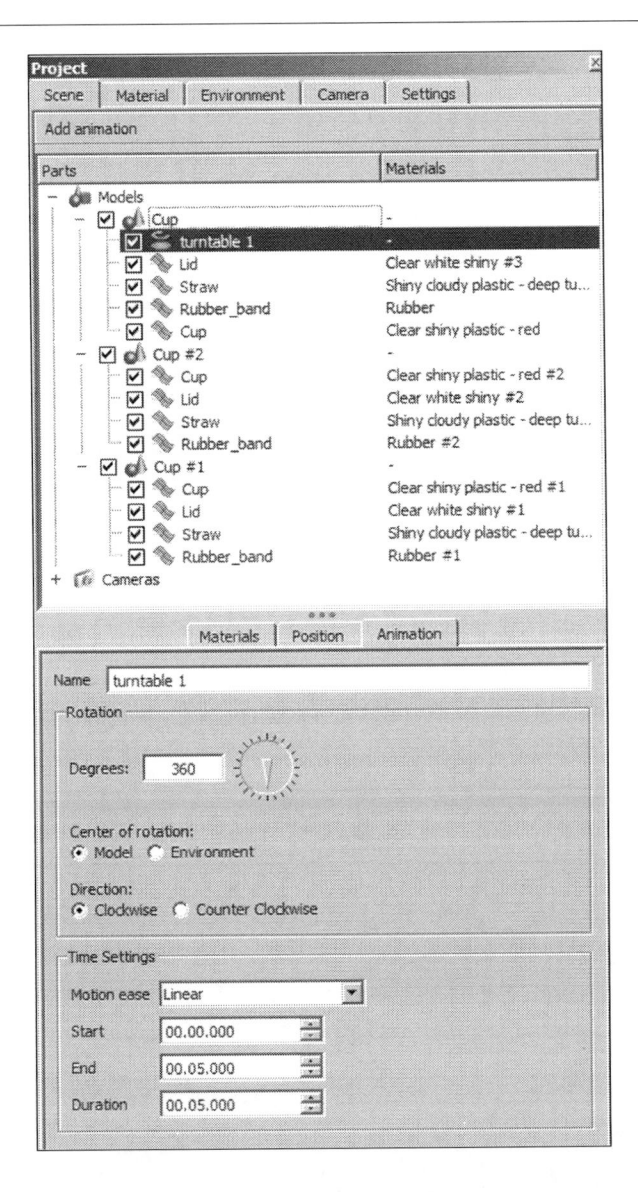

To create the desired look for our models, it is necessary to understand how we output our images. In conclusion, having a deeper understanding of the parameters and how they work in KeyShot can help us reduce rendering times, avoid modifying the wrong parameters, and permanently set up various rendering scenarios to speed up our workflow for future projects.

Summary

When adjusting the rendering samples in the Ouput menu inside Render options, do so by small increments and do render tests. Having high values will increase render time significantly. Render times are also affected by the resolution and print size. We recommend to use smaller resolution and size for testing purposes. Also it is preferably to use the Render Region feature if available. In the Quality menu of the Render options window, use smaller values for overall parameters, since the options found here affect our scene globally and hence, they affect our render time as well. We briefly discussed how easily we can create a turntable animation, which gives us another opportunity to present our work. As usual, practice using other models and choose other values for the parameters discussed in this chapter; this way we can learn and observe various results when combining different render settings and materials.

In our next chapter, we will learn how to add effects to our images using Photoshop when rendering them directly in KeyShot is not an option.

5
Adding Effects with Photoshop

In the following section, we are going to illustrate how to pose our final images to create the final stage of our renders. We are also going to learn some quick techniques and effects to enhance the look of our work, and we will be using Photoshop to add labels, create a vignette effect, and also replace the backplate of our model with a background of our own.

In this chapter you will learn:

- Replacing backgrounds
- Adding vignette effects
- Working with labels and letterings

Replacing our background

Sometimes it isn't an option to use a particular background for our renders. In such cases, adding an alpha channel to our final renders can be extremely helpful. By including the alpha channel with an image, KeyShot will render our model isolated from the background or backplate that is being used. To include an alpha channel with our images, we have to first choose a file format that is capable of accepting it. In our case, we have chosen the PNG file format because it supports an alpha channel and it preserves the quality of our images better than JPEG.

Adding Effects with Photoshop

There are also other file formats such as TIFF and EXR that support an alpha channel but these files are used for other situations such as printing or animation.

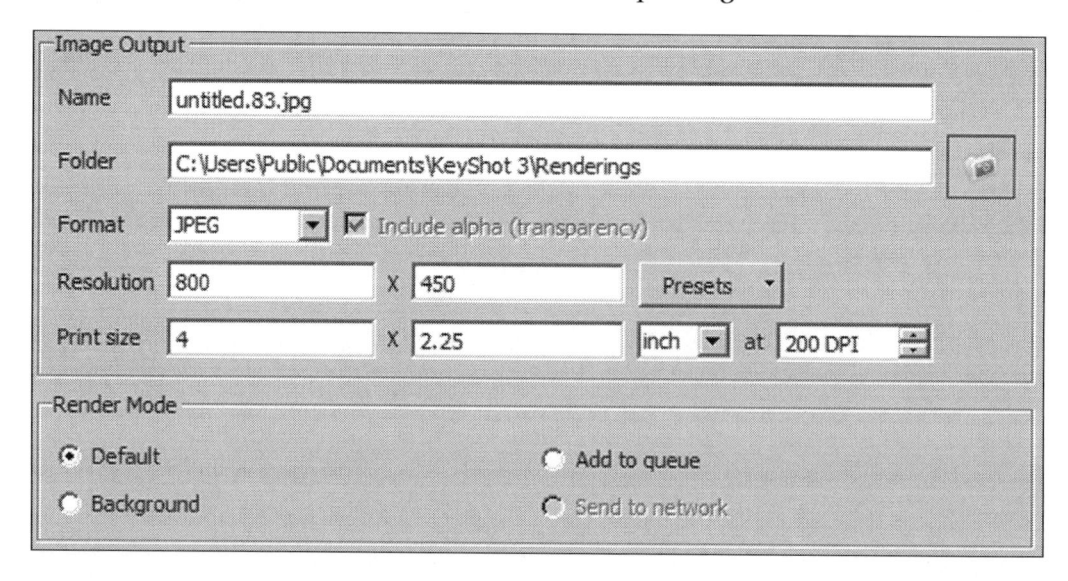

> The **Include alpha (transparency)** option is grayed out because we are using the JPEG file format and JPEG does not support an alpha channel, By selecting PNG format, this option will become available to us.

Continuing on from our Wacom lineup exercise, let's render our project by changing our file format into PNG and making sure the Include alpha (transparency) checkbox is checked. Once the figure is rendered:

1. Open Photoshop.
2. Create a new document by performing the following steps:
    1. Name the project to your preference.
    2. Adjust **Width** to `17`.
    3. Set **Height** as `11`.
    4. Set **Resolution** to `150`.
    5. Select the **Color** mode as `RGB`.
3. Click on **OK** to create a new document in Photoshop.

With the document opened, let's first add our background:

1. Select the **File** menu from Photoshop.
2. Choose the option **Place**.
3. Select the background **Back_1** and place it on our scene.

Now we are going to add our Wacom lineup model and place it on the scene. The model should be standing alone without a background since we rendered the image with an alpha channel.

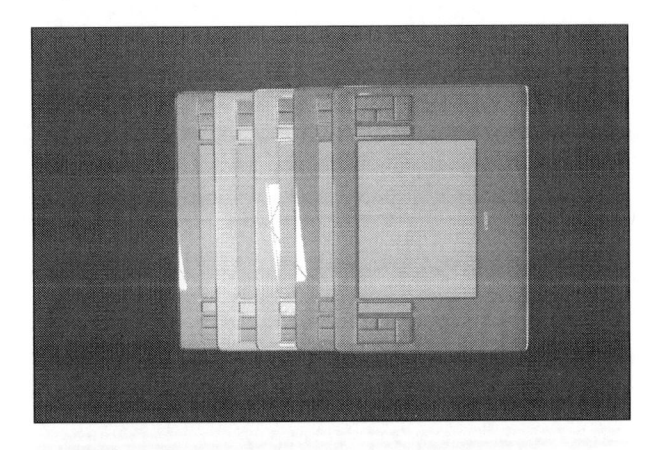

After the model has been placed on top of the background, let's drag it to make it larger, as in the example shown in the following screenshot:

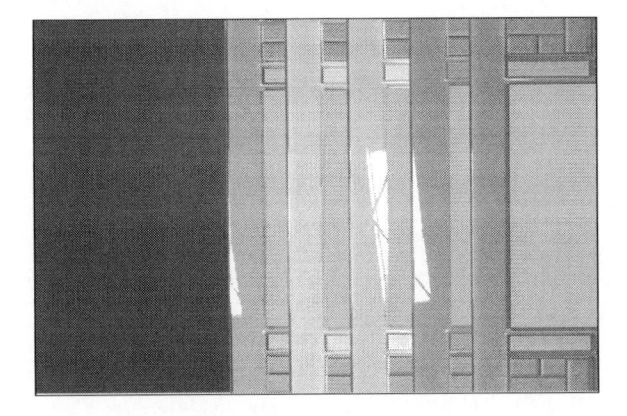

If we need to make color corrections or contrast adjustments, we can do so by going to the **Image** menu in Photoshop, where under the **Adjustment** category there are various options we can choose from. In this case, I added slightly more contrast to our Wacom lineup image and adjusted the blue tones.

Adding Effects with Photoshop

To create our vignette effect, let's first hide all our layers except our white background layer.

1. Create a new layer by clicking on **Layer | New | Layer** or by pressing the hot keys *Shift + Ctrl + N*.
2. Name the new layer as **Vignette**.
3. Pick a dark shade of gray for our foreground color.
4. Select our **Vignette** layer and fill our scene with the dark gray color.

5. Then select the **Marquee** tool.
6. On the top of the toolbar let's change the feather value to `120`.
7. The Feather tool helps to soften the edges selection made by the **Marquee** tool.
8. With the **Marquee** tool still selected, drag and create a rectangle selection. Since we have added `120` to the feather value, our rectangle selection now should have rounded edges.
9. Hit backspace to erase the selected region.
10. Now we should have our **Vignette** effect.
11. Turn the layers back on.

12. We can also add some lettering for our presentation.

Geek Supplier
For all art needs
(408)432-4412
www.GSpplier.com

Labels are images with an included alpha channel or transparency channel. In KeyShot, labels can be used as decals or stickers that can be placed anywhere in the model. We can create our own labels by saving our files with a transparency channel in Photoshop and then use them in KeyShot. The following steps show how to create a label:

1. Let's open our **Geek Supplier** image file by going to **File | Open | Geek Supplier** image sample.
2. Next, select the **Magic** tool, click and select all the boundaries around the letters of the **Geek Supplier** image, and make sure all the dark areas are selected.
3. Press *Ctrl + J* to create a new layer based on the selection.
4. Hide our first layer by clicking on the eye icon next to the layer.

5. Save our file in the PNG format.

As we can see in the previous screenshot, our newly created image has a transparent background that can be used in KeyShot or other applications.

Summary

What we showed in this chapter is just one way to showcase our work. Our goal was to create an image for advertising purposes. We created more versions of our Wacom tablet and changed its colors to add variety and we learned how to add a vignette effect and labels to our final image. We could have rendered out our vignette effect inside KeyShot, but that would have increased render times dramatically; for this reason we decided to add those effects using Photoshop. We recommend that any special effects such as Depth of Field, Vignette, or glows to be done outside of KeyShot since they considerably increase render time.

Lastly, we encourage readers to keep practicing using our cup and the bullet project to create different scenarios and to add the effects we learned in this chapter.

Command Lists and Hotkeys

Shortcuts menu
The shortcuts found here are also listed in KeyShot's hotkey menu list by pressing the *K* key for PCs and Macs.

Files and documents
The following are the shortcut keys related to files and documents:

- **Creating a new project**: *Ctrl + N*
- **Saving a project**: *Ctrl + S*
- **Saving the project as:**: *Ctrl + Alt + S*
- **Opening a project**: *Ctrl + O*
- **Closing KeyShot**: *Ctrl + Q*

Toggling
The following are the shortcuts keys related to toggling:

- **Full screen**: *F*
- **Activate toolbar**: *T*
- **Presentation mode**: *F*
- **KeyShot hotkey list**: *K*
- **Heads-up display**: *H*
- **Library**: Space bar

Space and environment

The following are the shortcut keys related to space and environment:

- **Rotate**: *Ctrl* + left mouse button, and then drag
- **Resetting position**: *Ctrl + R*
- **Setting to flat ground**: *G*
- **Setting background with color**: *C*
- **Setting background with backplate**: *B*
- **Setting background with HDRI**: *E*
- **Adjusting brightness to large**: Up and down arrows
- **Adjusting brightness to small**: Left and right arrows

Camera hotkeys

The following are the camera hotkeys:

- **Using perspective**: *Shift + Alt* + right mouse button, and then drag
- **Panning**: Middle mouse button, and then drag
- **Distancing**: Scroll wheel
- **Zooming**: *Alt* + scroll wheel
- **Tilting**: *Alt + Ctrl* + scroll wheel
- **Perspective**: *Shift + Alt* + right mouse button, and then drag
- **Tumbling**: Left mouse button, and then drag

General hotkeys

The following are the general hotkeys:

- **Undoing**: *Ctrl + Z*
- **Opening environment**: *Ctrl + E*
- **Opening backplate**: *Ctrl + B*
- **Importing a model**: *Ctrl + I*
- **Rendering menu**: *Ctrl + P*
- **Taking screenshot**: *P*

Material hotkeys

The following are the material hotkeys:

- **Editing material**: Double-click on the model using left mouse button
- **Selecting a material**: *Shift* + left mouse button
- **Applying selected material**: *Shift* + right mouse button
- **Applying copy material**: *Shift* + *Ctrl* + right mouse button

Animation hotkeys

The following are the animation hotkeys:

- **Timeline**: *A*
- **Playback**: *Shift* + Space bar

Real-time hotkeys

The following are the real-time hotkeys:

- **Using performance mode**: *Alt* + *P*
- **Toggling GI**: *I*
- **Toggling self shadows**: *S*
- **Pause**: *Shift* + *P*

Index

A

Add job button, queue menu 91
Adjustments tab, HDRI editor 60
Adjustment category 99
advanced material 44, 45
Alt + Ctrl + scroll wheel (tilting) 104
Alt + P (performance mode, using) 105
Alt + scroll wheel (zooming) 104
Alpha channel 97-99, 101
animation hotkeys
  A (timeline) 105
  Shift + Space bar (playback) 105
Animation Wizard icon 94
anti aliasing, quality menu 90
A (timeline) 105
Azimuth (Orbit) 70

B

background, replacing 97-101
Background section
  about 58
  backplate image option 58
  color option 58
  Lighting Environment option 58
backplate
  about 54
  opening 104
backplate image option 58
barrel, stylus 30
B (background setting with backplate) 104
Bloom intensity 64
box mapping method 37
brightness control 58
brightness parameter 63

bump channel, texture properties 39
bump map, insulated cup
  adding 75

C

camera
  about 72
  attributes 70
  Azimuth (Orbit) 70
  backplate, changing 67
  creating 70
  deleting 70
  Distance (Dolly) 70
  Focal Length attribute 72
  Inclination (Elevation) 71
  locking 70
  orthographic 72
  perspective 72
  setting up, for project 65, 66
  tablet, shadows 68, 69
  twist 72
  view, with orthographic mode 73
camera hotkeys
  about 104
  Alt + Ctrl + scroll wheel (tilting) 104
  Alt + scroll wheel (zooming) 104
  Left mouse button, and then drag
    (tumbling) 104
  Middle mouse button, and then drag
    (panning) 104
  Scroll wheel (distancing) 104
  Shift + Alt + right mouse button, and then
    drag (perspective) 104
  Shift + Alt + right mouse button, and then
    drag (perspective, using) 104

Camera property tab
  about 65
camera view, with orthographic mode 73
  Depth of Field option 73
  Focus distance option 73
  F-stop option 73
C (background setting with color) 104
Clear white shiny material 23
client unit, network menu 92
color option 58
color, texture properties 38
connector, stylus 31
contrast slider 57
Ctrl + Alt + S (project, saving as) 103
Ctrl + B (backplate, opening) 104
Ctrl + E (environment, opening) 104
Ctrl + I (model, importing) 104
Ctrl + left mouse button, and then drag 104
Ctrl + N (new project creation) 103
Ctrl + O (project, opening) 103
Ctrl + Q (KeyShot, closing) 103
Ctrl + R (reset position) 104
Ctrl + S (project, saving) 103
Ctrl + Z (undoing) 104
cylindrical, mapping method 38

D

delete job button, queue menu 91
Depth of Field option 73
depth parameter, labels tab 40
Diffuse attribute 88
diffuse modifier 33
diffuse transmission property 34
Distance (Dolly) 70
Double-click on the model using left mouse button (material, editing) 105

E

E (background setting with HDRI) 104
environment properties window 14
Environment tab
  about 13
  Background section 58
  categories 57
  Ground section 59
  Lighting section 57
  real-time settings section 62
eraser, stylus 29

F

F (full screen) 103
files and documents, shortcut keys
  Ctrl + Alt + S (project, saving as) 103
  Ctrl + N (new project creation) 103
  Ctrl + O (project, opening) 103
  Ctrl + Q (KeyShot, closing) 103
  Ctrl + S (project, saving) 103
flatten ground 59
Focal Length attribute 72
Focus distance option 73
format, output menu 90
F (presentation mode) 103
F-stop option 73

G

Gamma parameter 63
Geek Supplier image file 101
general hotkeys
  about 104
  Ctrl + B (backplate, opening) 104
  Ctrl + E (environment, opening) 104
  Ctrl + I (model, importing) 104
  Ctrl + P (menu, rendering) 104
  Ctrl + Z (undoing) 104
  P (screenshot, taking) 104
glass material 44
Global Illumination 64
global illumination quality, quality menu 90
ground grid 59
Ground Grid option 68
Ground section
  about 59
  flatten ground 59
  ground grid 59
  ground size 59
  shadow color 59
ground size 59
G (setting to flat ground) 104

H

HDRI editor
  about 60
  adjustments tab 61
  pins tab 61
hdri-locations_factory_4k environment file 87
HDRIs
  about 54
  loading, for scene 54, 55
H (heads-up display) 103
Hide Part option 88
high dynamic range imaging (HDRI) method 6, 23
hotkeys
  animation hotkeys 105
  camera hotkeys 104
  general hotkeys 104
  material hotkeys 105
  Real-time hotkeys 105
HyperShot. *See* **KeyShot**

I

Inclination (Elevation) 71
include alpha (transparency) option 98
index of refraction (IOR) 40
insulated cup
  about 74
  bump map, adding 75
  lighting, changing 78-80
  material, applying 75
  transparent colorless plastic, applying 78
intensity, labels tab 40
I (toggling GI) 105

K

Keep files in one folder option 86
Keep files in single folder option 66
KeyShot
  about 5
  camera, setting up 65
  hotkeys 104, 105
  insulated cup 74, 75
  lighting, working 51, 52

projects, importing 8, 9
rendering 5
render options 89
trial version downloading, URL for 7
versus traditional rendering programs 6, 7
K (KeyShot hotkey list) 103

L

label
  about 101
  adding 25
  creating, steps for 101
labels tab
  depth parameter 40
  index of refraction (IOR) 40
  intensity 40
  specualr property 40
  two sided checkbox 41
left and right arrows (brightness adding to small) 104
Left mouse button, and then drag (tumbling) 104
letterings 101
Library tab 11
lighting
  about 51
  adjusting 53, 54
  applying, to scene 53
  working 51
Lighting Environment option 58
Lighting section
  brightness control 58
  contrast slider 57
  height parameter 58
  rotation parameter 58
  size parameter 58
Lock Aspect checkbox 62

M

Magic tool 101
Marquee tool 100
master unit, network menu 92
Material Editor window 20
material hotkeys
  Double-click on the model using left mouse button (material, editing) 105

Shift + Ctrl + right mouse button (copy material, applying) 105
Shift + left mouse button (material, selecting) 105
Shift + right mouse button (selected material, applying) 105
material properties window 12, 13
materials
   about 18
   adding, to writing pad 18, 19
   advanced material 44, 45
   and properties 32, 33
   applying, for rubber pad 76
   applying, to barrel 30
   applying, to connector 31
   applying, to eraser 29
   applying, to insulated cup 75
   applying, to nib 31, 32
   applying, to rubber grip 30
   applying, to side switches 30
   applying 105
   creating 42
   diffuse modifier 33
   diffuse transmission property 34
   glass creating, plastic used 43
   glass material 44
   label, adding 25, 26
   labels tab 40
   metals 44
   plastics 42
   refraction index property 35
   roughness modifier 34
   selecting 105
   specular modifier 33
   specular transmission property 34
   tablet button 21
   tablet case 19, 20
   texture properties 35
   texturing 45-49
   transparent cover 22-25
   USB cable 26-28
Material tab 11
Material Template 9
metals 44
methods, texturing 45-49
Middle mouse button, and then drag (panning) 104

models
   duplicating 80, 81
   importing 104
   objects, duplicating 82
Move down button, queue menu 91
Move Object option 68, 88
Move up button, queue menu 91

N

network menu, render option
   about 92
   client unit 92
   master unit 92
   slave unit 92
nib, stylus 31, 32

O

objects, duplicating 82
opacity channel, texture properties 40
orthographic 72
output menu, render option
   about 90
   format 90
   print size 90
   render mode 90
   resolution 90

P

pad
   about 18
   writing 19
pins tab, HDRI editor 61
pixel filter size, quality menu 90
planar X, mapping method 35
planar Y, mapping method 36
planar Z, mapping method 36
plastics
   about 42
   used, for creating glass 43
print size, output menu 90
project
   environment properties window 14
   Environment tab 13
   importing 8, 9
   material properties window

about 12, 13
Material tab 11, 12
Scene tab 10
viewport 8
Project Editor window 22, 87
P (screenshot, taking) 104

Q

Quality and Performance modes 63
quality menu, render option
  anti aliasing 90
  DOF quality 91
  global illumination quality 90
  pixel filter size 90
  ray bounces 90
  samples 90
  shadow quality 91
  sharper texture filtering 91
  sharp shadows 91
queue menu, render option 91

R

Ray Bounces 63, 64
ray bounces, quality menu 90
Real-time hotkeys
  Alt + P (performance mode, using) 105
  I (toggling GI) 105
  Shift + P (pause) 105
  S (toggling self shadows) 105
real-time settings section
  about 62
  Brightness parameter 63
  Gamma parameter 63
  Global Illumination 64
  Lock Aspect checkbox 62
  Quality and Performance modes 63
  Ray Bounces 63, 64
  Self Shadows 64
  Shadow Quality 64
  Vignetting Strength 64
refraction index property 35
region menu, render option 92
render mode, output menu 90
render options, KeyShot
  about 89
  network menu 92

output menu 90
quality menu 90
queue menu 91
region menu 92
resolution, output menu 90
rotation parameter 58
roughness modifier 34
roughness parameter 18
rubber grip, stylus 30
rubber pad
  of cup, materials applying for 76

S

samples, quality menu 90
scale, texture properties 38
Scene tab 10
Scroll wheel (distancing) 104
Self Shadows 64
shadow color 59
shadow quality 64
shadow quality, quality menu 91
sharper texture filtering, quality menu 91
sharp shadows, quality menu 91
Shift + Alt + right mouse button, and then
    drag (perspective) 104
Shift + Alt + right mouse button, and then
    drag (perspective, using) 104
Shift + Ctrl + right mouse button
    (copy material, applying) 105
Shift + left mouse button (material,
    selecting) 105
Shift + P (pause) 105
Shift + right mouse button (selected
    material, applying) 105
Shift + Space bar (playback) 105
shift X, texture properties 38
shift Y, texture properties 38
shortcut keys
  animation hotkeys 105
  camera hotkeys 104
  files and document 103
  general hotkeys 104
  material hotkeys 105
  real-time hotkeys 105
  space and environment 104
  toggling 103
Show All Parts option 22

side switches, stylus 30, 31
size parameter 58
S key 64
slave unit, network menu 92
space and environment, shortcut keys
   B (background setting with backplate) 104
   C (background setting with color) 104
   Ctrl + left mouse button, and then drag 104
   Ctrl + R (reset position) 104
   E (background setting with HDRI) 104
   G (setting to flat ground) 104
   left and right arrows (brightness adding to small) 104
   up and down arrows (brightness adding to large) 104
space bar (library) 103
specualr property 40
specular box, texture properties 38
specular modifier 33
specular transmission property 34
spherical, mapping method 37
S (toggling self shadows) 105
stylus
   barrel 30
   connector 31
   eraser 29
   nib 31
   rubber grip 30
   side switches 30, 31

T

tablet
   button 21
   case 19, 20
   label, adding 25, 26
   transparent cover 22-25
   USB cable 26-28
T (activate toolbar) 103
texture properties
   box mapping method 37
   bump channel 39
   color 38
   cylindrical, mapping method 38
   mapping method 35
   opacity channel 40
   planar X, mapping method 35

planar Y, mapping method 36
planar Z, mapping method 36
position 35
scale 38
shift X 38
shift Y 38
specular box 38
spherical mapping 37
UV coordinates, mapping method 38
toggling, shortcut keys
   F (full screen) 103
   F (presentation mode) 103
   H (heads-up display) 103
   K (KeyShot hotkey list) 103
   space bar (library) 103
   T (activate toolbar) 103
traditional rendering programs
   high dynamic range imaging (HDRI) method 6
   points 7
   versus KeyShot 6
turntable presentation
   creating 93, 94
two sided checkbox, labels tab 41

U

up and down arrows (brightness adding to large) 104
USB cable 26-28
UV coordinates, mapping method 38

V

viewport
   model, moving 10
   model, rotating 10
   model, scaling 10
vignette effect, creating 100
Vignetting Strength 64

W

Wacom project
   setting up 85-89
Wacom stylus. *See* stylus
Wacom_tablet project 86
Width and Height field 62

Thank you for buying
KeyShot 3D Rendering

About Packt Publishing

Packt, pronounced 'packed', published its first book "*Mastering phpMyAdmin for Effective MySQL Management*" in April 2004 and subsequently continued to specialize in publishing highly focused books on specific technologies and solutions.

Our books and publications share the experiences of your fellow IT professionals in adapting and customizing today's systems, applications, and frameworks. Our solution based books give you the knowledge and power to customize the software and technologies you're using to get the job done. Packt books are more specific and less general than the IT books you have seen in the past. Our unique business model allows us to bring you more focused information, giving you more of what you need to know, and less of what you don't.

Packt is a modern, yet unique publishing company, which focuses on producing quality, cutting-edge books for communities of developers, administrators, and newbies alike. For more information, please visit our website: www.packtpub.com.

Writing for Packt

We welcome all inquiries from people who are interested in authoring. Book proposals should be sent to author@packtpub.com. If your book idea is still at an early stage and you would like to discuss it first before writing a formal book proposal, contact us; one of our commissioning editors will get in touch with you.

We're not just looking for published authors; if you have strong technical skills but no writing experience, our experienced editors can help you develop a writing career, or simply get some additional reward for your expertise.

[PACKT] PUBLISHING

Blender 2.5 Lighting and Rendering

ISBN: 978-1-84719-988-1   Paperback: 252 pages

Bring your 3D world to life with lighting, compositing, and rendering

1. Render spectacular scenes with realistic lighting in any 3D application using interior and exterior lighting techniques
2. Give an amazing look to 3D scenes by applying light rigs and shadow effects
3. Apply color effects to your scene by changing the World and Lamp color values

Cinema 4D R13 Cookbook

ISBN: 978-1-84969-186-4   Paperback: 514 pages

Elevate your art to the fourth dimension with Cinema 4D

1. Master all the important aspects of Cinema 4D
2. Learn how real-world knowledge of cameras and lighting translates onto a 3D canvas
3. Learn Advanced features like Mograph, Xpresso, and Dynamics.
4. Become an advanced Cinema 4D user with concise and effective recipes

Please check **www.PacktPub.com** for information on our titles

[PACKT] PUBLISHING

3ds Max Speed Modeling for 3D Artists

ISBN: 978-1-84969-236-6   Paperback: 422 pages

Flex your speed modeling muscles using 3ds Max

1. Learn to speed model in 3ds Max, with an emphasis on hard surfaces
2. Up to date coverage, covering 3ds Max 2013 features
3. Focused explanations with step-driven practical lessons balance learning and action

Final Cut Pro X Cookbook

ISBN: 978-1-84969-296-0   Paperback: 452 pages

Edit with style and ease using the latest editing technologies in Final Cut Pro X!

1. Edit slick, professional videos of all kinds – music videos, promos, documentaries, even feature films
2. Add hundreds of built-in animated titles, transitions, and effects without complicated keyframing
3. Learn tons of time-saving workflows to tricky, yet common editing scenarios
4. Fix common (and uncommon) sound and image issues with a click or two of the mouse

Please check www.PacktPub.com for information on our titles

Printed in Great Britain
by Amazon.co.uk, Ltd.,
Marston Gate.